*M*an *O*man

A Redhead in Arabia

BENITA STAFFORD-SMITH

iUniverse, Inc.
New York   Bloomington

Man Oman
A Redhead in Arabia

Copyright © 2010 Benita Stafford-Smith

iUniverse books may be ordered through booksellers or by contacting:

iUniverse
1663 Liberty Drive
Bloomington, IN 47403
www.iuniverse.com
1-800-Authors (1-800-288-4677)

ISBN: 978-1-4502-6213-2 (pbk)
ISBN: 978-1-4502-6214-9 (ebk)

Printed in the United States of America

iUniverse rev. date: 10/12/2010

Acknowledgments

First of all, thank you – *shukran* – to the wonderful people of Oman, whom you will meet in this book. Their kindness and friendship to a stranger in their land have made my experiences memorable.

And to Les Kletke, the manager of this book project, who made the extra effort to keep me writing. Always! In my early days in Muscat, Les's emails were gifts from God. Many times he was my only contact with the English-speaking world. His support during my first few months here was a life-saver. Thank you, Les, from the depths of my heart.

To Lois Braun, for her patience and guidance as editor. It is no easy task to work with someone you have never met and lives on the other side of the world. Thanks, Lois – I feel I have gained a new friend.

Thanks to my cousin Pat Letendre for her keen eye in editing, her sage advice on writing and publishing, and her infinite wisdom and support.

Shukran to my friends and family who came to visit me in Oman during my first year. I was so proud to show off my new home and share my discoveries. Their support and love were also gifts from God, my angels. Thank you.

To those friends and loved ones, too numerous to mention, who encouraged me from afar: shukran. They encouraged me to follow this path to Oman, to explore and discover, and most importantly, to overcome the inevitable obstacles that are a part of life anywhere.

To my sister, Wendy whom you will meet later, for her love and updates that keep me connected to "home".

To my Dad for his persistence in getting me on the phone and keeping in touch.

And lastly, to my dear departed Mom who, although not here physically, is always with me in spirit. Her continuous support of a daughter who chooses the path less travelled always was and continues to be a constant source of inspiration. Shukran, Mom.

Contents

Prologue. ix

New culture, new environment 1

Getting settled. 9

About marriage, and a wedding 15

Red tape and driving 22

My new Omani friends 29

Residence card blues. 33

A visit home. 39

Destinations. 44

The Bollywood Dance. 50

Late fall, and storm at sea 56

Round the bend' 61

The crystal ball and Eid 65

India! 71

The New Year, and visitors from Saskatoon 81

Middle East news and expat culture 87

A trip to Thailand 94

Again, the goat 101

Dubai, and Arabian nights 105

Epilogue. 111

About the Author 115

Prologue

How did I get here? The question struck me as I sat one day in the living room of a country home belonging to an Omani gentleman; more specifically, the country home of the gentleman's Wife Number One. I was surrounded by women dressed in their traditional apparel, their heads covered, but not their faces. Young children ran and played around us, speaking a language I could not understand. Wife Number Two and her family were across the way in their villa. A swimming pool between the two homes is shared by both families. Am I really here?

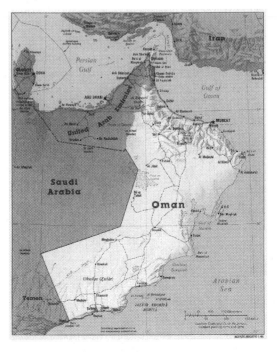

Yes, I really am here. Oman is a small country in the Middle East. I live in Muscat, a city that is five km wide and sixty km long, having been built between the mountains and the Sea of Arabia. The beauty of the people and the country often takes my breath away.

What would my mother think? She passed away a year-and-a-half before I came here, and I still often feel her presence. When she was alive, she was my number one supporter, but I believe my living in Muscat, Oman, in the Middle East, would be a big stretch for her. Yet I feel her loving support often in this part of the world. If she were still alive and healthy, I would bring her to Oman for a visit and show her this beautiful, peaceful, gentle country. She would like it. Once, I heard my Dad, who is still alive, joke about coming to visit me. I was surprised, as Dad rarely leaves "the farm," as he would call it. (In reality, "the farm" is five acres of land out in the country, in Manitoba, Canada. Mom was a gardener and Dad has been able to keep her gardens alive and verdant.) I lived in Saskatchewan for sixteen years and Dad came to visit twice, a ten-hour drive. I would be very surprised if he'd come to Oman, a seventeen-hour plane ride to the other side of the world.

But here I am. My mom once said to my sister that I was a bit of a nomad, never really settling down, and she was right. The years I spent raising my son alone were probably the most settled years of my life. But my son has finished university, and has become a grown man of whom I am very proud.

So it's my time now. When I began planning my move, I was not sure where I would end up, but I hoped, and continue to hope, to travel and to experience all that life has to offer in different parts of the world. I love adventure!

I'm often asked how I ended up in Muscat. Before I came, I'd spent the previous eight years building my business: coaching clients, speaking professionally, and writing. I was fortunate to have many clients in Canada and the US, and felt blessed and privileged for the opportunity to work with them. People often ask, what kind of coaching do you do? Simply, I work with business people, helping them identify and develop their strengths to fulfil their dreams. Every case is different. The analogy often used is that of Tiger Woods. As a professional golfer, he had a coach whose job it was to only observe from a distance and provide insight into the strengths and weaknesses of his client. Tiger Woods wished to continually improve. My clients are accomplished people who want to continually improve and be the best that they can be.

In December of 2006, at the Canadian Association of Professional Speakers Conference in Ottawa, I attended a session on speaking internationally. The facilitator of the session lit a spark in me, a desire to work and travel around the world. Then in June of 2007, I attended a conference in Dubai on building a speaking business in the Gulf Coast Countries (GCC). After that eye-opening experience, I felt inspired to take the leap. November, 2007: I received an email from a friend, forwarded from a gentleman – a Dr. Mohammed – whom she had met while taking a course. He was looking for someone who was a professional speaker and a business coach who might be interested in moving to Oman to provide those services there. Was I interested?

When? Where? Really? Who is this man? They need a coach and a speaker? My intuition told me that the venture was right up my alley.

But what kind of country is Oman? Do the people speak English? What about the status of women? Do I want to go there? Why would I?

Yes, I had a million questions back then. I was ready. Or so I thought. (Are you ever really ready?) When I got that email in November, I had to confront the question. I decided that the best thing to do was to pursue the opportunity and see what happened. I replied to the email: yes, I was interested. Dr. Mohammed responded by telling me he would like to speak with me. After a lengthy telephone call, a strong connection formed between us.

The next step was a face-to-face meeting. He lives in Toronto for part of the year and in Oman for the rest. It just so happened I was on my way to speakers' conference in December and had a three-hour lay-over in Toronto. We met, and the bond was cemented. Dr. Mohammed would be on his way to Oman shortly and was hoping to close several contracts, which would form the basis of the Achievement Centre, his new coaching-and-training company in the Middle East. I was excited and nervous at the same time. But I'd have to wait and see if he got the business up and running or not.

Dr. Mohammed Benayoune is originally from Algeria and speaks three languages: English, French and Arabic. He came to Muscat from the UK as a professor of chemical engineering at Sultan Qaboos University. When he speaks of Oman and the opportunities he was given here, you can see the pride and admiration in his eyes. After his years at university, Mohammed joined the Ministry of Oil and Gas as an advisor. He had the opportunity to be involved from the beginning in the development of some of the sultanate's projects. Mohammed often shares with us his experiences of being the CEO of three petrochemical corporations at the same time, an exercise in very disciplined time management and leadership. One of the insights he gained during this period was that you can spend millions on buildings and equipment, but what makes or breaks the success is the people. This led him to acquire the rights to the Achievement Centre for the Middle East, providing complete talent management services in Oman. Mohammed comes to Oman for extended periods of time dedicated to business development. He is very well connected in the Oman business community.

The email arrived in January, 2008: he was close to finalizing the deal and wanted to know how serious I was. I had to send my answer: *Yes!*

In February, the contracts were concluded, and I was ready to go. I am a firm believer in the power of intention. Intention also needs action. Intention + action = results. I was on my way to Muscat, Oman.

Jackey Backman and I had worked together in Canada for a few years delivering seminars for a US-based seminar company. Every couple of months, we used to travel together for a few weeks from Halifax to Vancouver, stopping at a different city ever day. In addition, we both continued to run our own businesses.

We were instant friends and really enjoyed the time we spent together. Jackey lived in Rockwood, a small town in southern Ontario, about an hour-and-a-half from Toronto. When I was working in the Toronto area, I would often stop at her home. I was lucky enough to meet her family on several occasions: her husband Fredrick, who emigrated from Sweden; their two wonderful sons, Eric and Jonathon; and her parents, who came originally from Malta.

When I was in Toronto getting certified in the programs I would be delivering in the Middle East, I had dinner with Jackey one evening. I just happened to mention that Dr. Mohammed was still looking for another person for this assignment. Her eyes immediately lit up as she contemplated this thought. She said she would talk to Fred that night. A few hours after we parted, I received an email from Jackey: "Fred wants to know when we should start packing." I think their connections with Malta and Sweden influenced their decision; they decided they wanted the children to have an international outlook. My friend would be going with me to Oman!

I closed my private coaching practice in Canada and left Winnipeg, Manitoba, with one month's notice. There was little time for preparation; or, you could say that I had been preparing for this move in my dreams for a couple of years. Dreams do come true. I gave away everything I owned and left for Muscat with two suitcases. It was a very freeing experience. (I try to avoid collecting things while I'm here in Oman, but that's proving to be difficult.)

And so I began my work in Muscat, delivering the Results Centred Leadership program to senior executives in the oil and gas industry. My clients were to be Omanis, ready to learn new ways to lead their companies and country in the global economy. In case you haven't figured it out yet, I am passionate about my work. I feel blessed to be a leadership coach, giving training sessions and working one-on-one with those clients.

They are wonderful people; getting to know them is proving to be such a gift for me.

We've arrived!

New culture, new environment

We arrived at the Muscat airport after a gruelling seventeen-hour trip from Toronto. It was close to midnight. We were looking forward to sleeping in a comfortable bed and having a hot meal the next day.

We had brought a lot of materials with us for the business, so it took a while to clear customs. To our surprise, we were met by Mohammed's brother Yacine, driving a Mercedes-Benz, and our contact Talal, driving a Jaguar. Both of those gentlemen were very easy on the eyes and we were thinking, Muscat is looking pretty good! Their welcome was generous and heart-felt. Yacine had brought food to our hotel room so we could have tea and a snack. What a wonderful arrival!

Yacine and his family would be moving to Canada in a few weeks, but he was able to show us a bit of Muscat and help us out on our first weekend here. Yacine was a great help to us and the kindness and integrity that Mohammed displays is obviously a family value, as Yacine possesses those qualities also. After that, Talal became our lifesaver. He helped us to get settled. Talal is Jordanian, as are his wife and five children. He would often laugh as he took us to the grocery store and furniture shopping, saying his wife would be jealous, as she normally had a hard time getting him to do shopping of any kind. A few weeks later, we would meet Talal's family.

I spent the first few weeks in an apartment hotel where I was waited on hand and foot, and regularly addressed by the staff as "Madam." At first I was affronted by being called that. In Canada, the term *ma'am* is often used in a disparaging sort of way, as in, "I'm sorry, *Ma'am*, but you can*not* bring that dog in here!" But I have come to accept being referred to as *madam* in Oman. The honorific is just one aspect of the luxury services offered in Arab countries. Everyone I've met has been friendly and helpful. Fortunately, most Omanis speak English as well as their native tongue.

1

Trying to remember names was challenging, since they were unfamiliar to me – Yacine, Talal, Saif. Of course, Mohammed and Ali are common names. But I had difficulty pronouncing some of the others. As I worked with clients, I found I steadily got the hang of it. At first, I struggled with putting the right face with the right name, too, especially when there were several Mohammeds in the room at once.

To add to the confusion, the spelling of a name can vary from day to day, situation to situation: Yaqoob is sometimes spelled Yaqoub, Salim/Salem, Majid/Majed, Adil/Adel, etc. It's common for vowels to be interchanged willy-nilly. And names are fascinating there for other reasons. Men incorporate the names of their fathers and grandfathers in their own names, along with the tribe name. And the tribe name, which is the surname, is also spelled differently in English, exchanging various vowels. Now, having taken Arabic language classes, I understand this exchange of vowels. In Arabic, there are only three vowels – a, u, and i – which explains the problems in translation of the names.

Despite Oman being mostly desert, a great variety of flowers beautify the city – familiar flowers: petunias, marigolds, hyacinths. It was odd to see those flowers growing in sand, when I thought of the effort we put into our gardens back home, making sure the soil mix is right, following a strict watering regimen. I've noticed at some of the luxury resorts in Muscat that a darker mixture is put in with the sand, and I'm assuming it's some kind of potting compound. The trees are loaded with colourful blooms, in stark contrast to the white and sandy colours on most of the buildings. The effect is stunning.

I was surprised, too, at how warm the waters of the Arabian Sea are. You can just walk right in, without observing the Canadian ritual of dipping first the toe of one foot in, then the other foot, all the while complaining and shivering and rubbing your torso and upper arms with handfuls of arctic waters. In Oman, you can walk a fair way out before the water begins to feel cool to the skin. One day, after floating and swimming in the salty sea, I went for a long walk along the beach. I had to keep my feet in the water, however, because the sand was incredibly hot. When I finished my stroll, I had to run up to the shade of the palm trees because the soles of my feet were burning. Later, I saw the locals walking to the shoreline with their sandals on and then removing them a few feet from the water. Good idea!

Oman has around 1200 km of beaches. The ones at the resort hotels are raked – not a speck of debris would dare to be visible. The public beaches are clean, too, but not as pristine as at the resorts. One of the beaches we were at, a popular spot with the Omanis, still showed signs of damage from a *gonu* (cyclone) that struck the area the previous summer. Crews were reconstructing the road system near that beach, making it difficult to get to. The shops and restaurants there were still closed. The gonu devastated the region. Reconstruction is on-going.

One night I went to a restaurant at Al Quorm beach to have supper. I ran into a gentleman from the UK. He was in Oman working on the construction of a new project called Blue City – hotels, luxury apartments, a golf course, a shopping centre. He mentioned that the beaches out towards Seeb are spectacular, with miles and miles of unspoiled shoreline. I knew I would have to check it out one day.

Seeking out other vacation possibilities, Jackey and I made a day-trip to Shangri-La, a complex of three five-star resorts built on the edge of a mountain overlooking the Arabian Sea. What a beautiful and serene retreat! To get there, you drive through the mountains for about twenty minutes, so it is relatively remote. The panoramic vista is breathtaking. It is a tourist destination and has a spa with a very good reputation for its luxurious services and facilities. I believe there are thirteen restaurants in the resort complex.

I hate to admit it, but I miss the big-box stores. Finding a place to buy office supplies when we arrived was aggravating. Seemed simple enough – go pick up markers, flip-chart paper, sticky-tack for the walls, and file folders. Not so. The first stationery supply store we went to did not have flip-chart paper, but the owner directed us to a store in a different part of town where flip-chart paper was in stock, a store he just happened to also own. So off we went. Have I mentioned there are no street signs or maps here? Did I mention we were on foot? When we asked directions, people pointed vaguely and said, "Over there." After many "over theres," we finally found the store. What seemed a simple task took an hour, an hour of walking in the draining heat of the afternoon. However, we were successful in acquiring everything except the file folders – lots of folders with two-hole fasteners, but no plain old 8.5x11 file folders. Not sure what people do here for filing, but I'm guessing they punch holes in everything. Way too much work for me. We purchased a sad, flimsy semblance of folders, which came in two choices of colours: pink or blue. A supply of proper file folders is one of the items I often ask my visitors to bring from Canada.

I never thought I'd say this, either, but I also sorely miss the convenience of Canada Post – go to any drugstore, get stamps, and drop your mail into conveniently located mailboxes. In Oman there is no door – to door mail delivery, postal outlets are few and far between, and post office boxes are a real rarity. The postal outlets are open only a limited time. It seemed every time I needed to access one, it was closed. I discovered eventually that you can rent a PO box to receive mail, but those are difficult to come by. Fortunately for us, the company that was hired to help us get settled, had a PO box, and Talal suggested we use it. Still makes me grateful for email, though.

Public washrooms are also bewildering to the newcomer. Each cubicle is completely enclosed, top to bottom, a little room that houses, besides the toilet, a water spigot and a drain in the floor. The floor and the walls are often drenched. Obviously, the personal habits of Arab women are different from what we're used to. If I was in a public place with a group of non-Arab friends or colleagues, one of the women was sent to the ladies' room as a scout, to suss out the conditions of the stalls. It was such a treat to find a clean, dry toilet with a toilet seat. Many places remove the seat. I have been told that the women stand on the toilet. I cannot fathom this; imagine trying to balance yourself on a toilet with no seat! And bathroom tissue is non-existent in most places; I always carry my own supply of toilet paper.

We were able to find two English-language daily newspapers in Muscat, the *Times* and the *Tribune*. They are set up like most newspapers, with news from the nation and its various regions front and foremost, but featuring items from India, Asia, and Europe as well. The Americas receive the least amount of coverage. News from Canada is rare and undetailed. When I lived in Canada, I didn't pay much attention to what was going on in the Gulf coast countries, but now that I am living here I find that I am hungry for news of the other Gulf countries. Frequently, reading the papers sends me to the Internet to research the locales mentioned. On weekends I like to pick up the *Gulf News*. In it you see virtually hundreds of job listings, offering generous salaries. In the earlier days, I faithfully scoured those listings, hoping to find something suitable for my son, who was thinking of coming to live in Oman.

As well, we could choose between two English radio stations. Both of them favour hip-hop and rap music, but I listen anyway. The newer of the two sends me into hysterical laughter at times. Hearing an announcer reading English copy and pronouncing Arabic names with a heavy French accent can be quite comical. The announcers on the other, older station tend to be British, but I couldn't say I understand them any better. (Many Omanis have been educated in the UK and speak with pleasant British accents.)

I was relieved to discover that the food is excellent. Most restaurants serve Indian, Iranian, or Lebanese food. Fresh fruits and vegetables are in abundance. But surprise!—no salad dressing. People from Oman who travel in or emigrate to North America must be terribly disappointed with the processed food served in restaurants in that part of the world. After we'd been in Oman for a while, Jackey and I went to a mall one day – a typical Western-type mall – and decided to drop in at a Chili's chain restaurant for a western meal. It was then that we realized we did not miss that kind of food at all. There are several restaurant chains in Muscat, including one we'd never heard of before: the Automatic Restaurants, which, despite the name, offer wonderful food. They make an "Automatic cocktail" that we fell in love with, a concoction of six different kinds of fresh fruits and fresh-squeezed juices.

We went to a fabulous restaurant called Karjeen's one evening. I ordered a dish called, simply, grilled chicken. It was served in an ornate silver brazier, complete with live coals. I found it difficult to eat the chicken, as it kept falling through the grill when I tried to cut it. The meat was delicious, tender and moist, with a tangy yet sweet sauce. I enjoyed the chicken so much I didn't mind the struggle. After I finished eating I looked around to discover many tables with those ornate grills on them, except that diners were taking the chicken pieces off the brazier and cutting it on their plates. I had a good laugh at myself.

The LuLu Hypermarket is the local supermarket. The place is huge. The whole first floor is just groceries. On the second level are electronics, clothing, jewellery, toys, and home furnishings, along with specialty shops: a newsstand, a mobile and Internet outlet, a small computer store, a coffee shop. One week the grocery department held a Mango Celebration, featuring 143 varieties of mangos. Imagine – 143 different kinds of mangos! I managed to try about ten and was surprised at how different they were, some sweet some tart. The word *lulu* means *pearl* in Arabic, and I can guess where the term *hyper* came from: at night, the building is lit up with dazzling neon, and it's a very busy place on weekends. The store was one of the first places Jackey and I learned to drive to when we got our rental car. We were so proud to be able to find our way to LuLu, and back to the hotel again without getting lost. It was one of the early victories in our adventures as newcomers.

I was most pleased to learn that tea is popular here, a result of the East Indian influence. Lipton Yellow Label is the standard tea served, but many places offer a good variety of black and green teas. You have to ask for "masala chai" in the local restaurants if you want the spicy chai tea we know in Canada; otherwise, the waiters will bring you a boring black tea. I found it comforting, after a long day spent navigating the new and the strange, to sit down to a familiar custom. All is right with the world when you can take a quiet moment with a cup of tea. After all the years of living in a coffee-drinking society, it was a pleasure to be in a tea-drinking society. Interesting that tea here is always served with warm milk – unexpected, especially in a hot climate, but such a nice touch.

One day, while giving a training session to twenty-two people, the "tea boy" appeared mid-afternoon to serve us our afternoon cup of tea – another delightful custom of the region. The concept may sound politically incorrect, but it's yet another of the luxuries enjoyed by Omanis. These men bring you tea, coffee, water, and snacks all day long at work. You only need ask and they are there. I noticed that use of a tea boy was standard practice at my clients' offices. (Coffee is available, but it's considered to be a "special request.")

A few interesting facts:

If your car is dirty in Oman, the police fine you twenty-five Omani rials, or $75 Canadian. Needless to say, all vehicles in Oman are immaculately clean.

Weekends are Thursday and Friday. Wednesday nights have a whole new meaning here, as does Monday, which is now Hump Day.

One activity that made us giggle like schoolgirls the first few times was filling the car up with gas. Gasoline prices here are subsidized by the Sultan and haven't been raised in a very long time. To fill up the gas tank in 2009 costs four Omani rials, or $12 – a special perk of living in a Gulf country.

Among our first social occasions here was a gathering of expats (expatriates) on a Thursday night (Thursday night=Saturday night). The couple hosting the gathering was originally from Calgary. They had been travelling for the past twelve years with their three children, living in Indonesia, Australia, and now Oman. Also present at the party were an American gentleman and his wife, who was Australian. They had recently moved from Saudi Arabia. Completing the guest list were a French-Canadian lady from Montreal, who married an Omani and had been living here for twenty-five years; a woman from the UK who had been in Oman for twenty years; and Jackey and myself.

Oman is a Muslim country, and Muslims traditionally do not consume liquor. If given a gift of alcohol, they will throw it away. They are not even allowed to re-gift it. To my surprise, expats need a license to consume liquor in their homes. Jackey and I had initially thought of stopping and buying a bottle of wine to take with us, but had no clue where to get one. As it turned out, we would not have been able to purchase the wine anyway, without a license or a letter from our sponsor.

I was taken aback, though, when I saw Omanis drinking in hotel bars, or at expat functions. I heard someone say that those Arabs consider themselves to be "modern Muslims," meaning they drink and smoke. Interesting definition of the term *modern*.

But no matter how different things are, the more they are the same. At the hotel I first stayed at, the Internet was down for three days while a new computer system was being installed. It was as frustrating there as it would be in any part of the world.

Have I mentioned how seductive the Arabian nights are? After the scorching heat of day, the clear, starry skies, the fragrance of flowers, and the tropical breezes are warm and inviting.

My new flat, first floor.

Getting settled

Shopping is not one of my favourite pastimes. However, to set up a new household I had to resign myself to it. Learning to shop in Oman offered an incredible opportunity.

I found a two-bedroom apartment that was large by Canadian standards, but small for Oman. The rooms in most homes and apartments are very spacious, with high ceilings and marble floors. With the extreme heat during summer, the large rooms are necessary for air circulation. May I just add that there are no closets? Anywhere?

Most people here live in large villas. The kitchens in traditional Omani homes are outside, in a separate building, so the smell of food won't permeate the rest of the house. Four or five bedrooms are the norm and every bedroom has its own bathroom. A master bedroom is typically large enough to hold a dance in. (But did I mention there are no closets?) The guest bathroom is situated close to the *guest* living room. Yes, villas have a special living room used only when guests are at the house. In traditional Omani homes you'll find that the ladies and gents have separate living rooms. Not only do all those cavernous rooms require many pieces of furniture to fill them, the furnishings have to be large. In other words, in Oman, size matters.

And that presented a bit of a problem when I went furniture shopping for my humble abode. The bedroom set I chose consisted of a super – king – sized bed, a six – section wardrobe, a dresser with mirror, a chest of drawers, and two night tables. (The price of furniture here is very reasonable. The master bedroom set was 550 Omani rials, about $1300, and included the mattress.) Try as I might, I was not able to fit it all in my bedroom. It was pretty close, though. One of the night tables ended up gracing the front hallway, covered with a very sparkly table cover and some traditional Omani glassware. You'd never know it was a night table.

In my apartment, the living room and dining room were combined. I had also seen that in villas, but again, my quarters were not that spacious. Living room furniture tends to come in standard sets consisting of a three-seater couch, a two-seater, two large armchairs, and three occasional tables. Dining room sets typically include six or eight chairs and a large buffet. (Remember, closets and storage space are rare). To my good fortune, I was able to find in one of the furniture stores a grouping called a "tea set," which had two large armchairs and a coffee table. At one of the Swedish import stores, I found a single couch for sale. Success!

There are many expats residing in Oman, and in June, many of them move elsewhere. (June seems to be the common time for contracts to expire.) The expats who are leaving put up signs in the stores and malls selling their furniture. Because I moved in May, I missed the opportunity to get in on some good deals. However, when Jackey moved out of my apartment in June to her own place, I managed to furnish my spare room and office with second-hand expat items for under one hundred Omani rials. Buying new would have been close to 1,000 OR (around $2,600 Canadian).

More frustrations followed, however.

When the washing machine was delivered, I discovered that installation was not included. That left the washing machine sitting in the middle of kitchen. I had purchased an *automatic* washing machine, quite the luxury here, as most people apparently use a manual type of machine where you must change the cycles manually, drain the water, and move the clothes into the spin basket. No dryers are required; you just hang your clothes up for an hour or two and voila! the job is done.

Getting back to the washing machine: I'd bought a used cooker (as stoves are called here) from Mohammed's brother, Yacine, who was moving to Canada. When the cooker was delivered earlier, my boss Mohammed brought two large propane tanks with it. Yes, propane. There is no infrastructure in Oman – no sewer and water, no gas. There is electricity, however. But the stove is run off large propane tanks. I hadn't noticed, but apparently all houses have tanks outside. Unfortunately, both my tanks were empty. Reikshan, the caretaker, took one of the tanks and had it filled. The other tank was sitting outside on the utility balcony. When the washing machine arrived, I moved the spare propane tank from the utility balcony to the kitchen area to make room for the washing machine out on the balcony. But the washing machine did not fit through the door because of the packaging. The delivery guys were not about to unpack it and put it outside on the balcony for me. I found that odd, since most people in the service industry here are helpful to a fault. For days, my washing machine and the propane tank sat in the middle of my kitchen like two, sad orphans.

In the kitchen and each bathroom there is a sewer drain. The trucks – I always call them honey wagons – come and empty out the septic tanks on a regular basis. You know when they arrived – you can smell it! Not a pleasant odor. I first observed this at the hotel. Then I noticed that all the homes have a valve coming out of their walls for the trucks to hook up to.

When my cell phone was dead and I wanted to charge the battery, I couldn't plug the phone itself into the charger and make calls. The charger seemed to be able to perform only one function at a time. That was inconvenient on Appliance Day for three reasons: 1. I couldn't call someone to come and install the washer, 2. the fridge was supposed to be delivered, but the store couldn't reach me, and, 3. I was waiting for a call back on the car I wished to purchase. The phone was dead – *aargh!!*

Then I couldn't install my mobile wireless Internet connection because it wouldn't recognize the Sim card – double *aargh!*

Back to the necessity of shopping: I needed to purchase essentials for the apartment. There were two items I've always considered common household tools – a cutlery tray and dishcloths. No so in Oman. My cutlery sat loose in a drawer and I was using a sponge to wash dishes. Cutlery trays and dishcloths continued to elude me, even though I had searched several different stores in pursuit of them. Couldn't find Scotch tape either. Rather puzzling. I would have thought Scotch tape was universal.

Oh-my-god, that man just stuck a ten-inch knife blade into the electrical outlet! I'm closing my eyes, I cannot watch this! A few seconds of terror pass and then I hear Reikshan's gentle voice saying, "It is okay now, Madam."

The electrical outlets in buildings here are standard European three-prong outlets. Many electrical appliances in Oman, however, have two-prong plugs. The solution is to push down the ground wire in the electrical outlet, which frees up the plug, and a two-prong appliance can easily be connected. It's typical to use the end of a pen for that job – a little perilous, I thought, but apparently safe; after all, it is the ground wire. At least, that is the logical voice in my head trying to accept the habit. If a pen is not available, then a knife is the next utensil of choice. The outlet itself does have a switch to turn power on and off to the plug. Most people simply stick the knife in even though the switch controlling the power supply to the outlet is ON.

My fear is rooted in my past, when I used to bake my own whole wheat bread. The bread did not rise all that well, resulting in small slices. When I made toast, I had to put a knife in the toaster and dig out the slices. And I remember my mother's warnings: *Unplug that toaster, you're going to electrocute yourself!* If she were alive, I can just image what she would say to this man sticking a knife in the electrical socket.

One of the things I love about this country is the service. There is always someone willing and able to help you. If you need assistance, you simply tell someone and the next thing you know, you have contact information. The day I moved into my apartment, Jackey was away on a business trip, so I was alone. At the hotel, I had the porter help me load up the car. But when I got to the apartment, I had to I make ten trips up the stairs, two of them carrying some pretty heavy luggage. Hard to believe we had accumulated that much stuff in just two weeks. I went back to the hotel later in the afternoon to take one more carload. Again, the hotel porter helped. When I mentioned how heavy some of the items were – did I intend for it to be a hint? – he offered to come to my flat to help. He informed the front desk of his intentions and off we went. What a luxury! He apologized for not availing himself sooner; he thought I had someone assisting at the other end. It was a good lesson for me. I had to learn to ask for help, that it's okay to stand back and let others assist you. Being an independent sort of person, I found the custom a little challenging.

The night I brought my new car home, the caretaker asked if Jackey and I would like a man to come every day and wash our cars for us. The cost: six Omani rials a month, or $15. I quickly got used to this lifestyle! My maid comes twice a week for a cost of approximately $35 per month. We were told it's a very high wage. Getting used to the pay scale here was a bit of a struggle for me. Talal, the man who helped us to settle in Muscat, kept telling us we must stop giving people so much money for their help. Giving a payment of five rials ($12) for a couple of hours labour is considered very extravagant. Most of the people doing those jobs make five rials a day, or even less. I continued to be extravagant with my tips, a practice which identified me to the locals as a Canadian. My sponsor here teased me about it one day, saying, "You will soon have more friends than you know what to do with!" Long gone were the days of lugging groceries and shopping items up the stairs. For a very small fee there was always someone quickly available to help.

I was so grateful for air-conditioning. How did people survive here in the days before AC? One night, when Jackey was still living with me, we returned from dinner to an apartment block with no electrical power. It had been out for over an hour in our area. The temperature at 9 PM was 36oC and the humidity was climbing. Walking outside from the car, my glasses fogged up! My apartment was on the third floor and it felt like a sauna. I sat on the floor quietly sweating. Such weather is good for the skin, I'm sure – no need to pay for a facial. No need for "hot yoga" here, either – just turn off the air-conditioning. Fortunately, the power went back on about ten minutes after our return, though it seemed a lot longer.

In the summer, the daytime temperatures reach 52oC. The evenings cool off nicely to between 28o and 30o, and there is often a very gently breeze blowing. I now understand the beauty of Arabian nights. But even so, we often laughed when we came out of a store or restaurant in the evening; we'd get hit by what felt like a blast furnace. We always said, "Who turned on the heat?"

Jackey's husband Fred and their two boys were scheduled to arrive in Muscat in mid-summer, so Jackey was very busy the months of June and July finding accommodations for her family and then furnishing them. She found the perfect four-bedroom flat in the outskirts of Muscat – plenty of room for the family, even though it meant a long drive to work for her. It was the upper floor of a brand new villa, very nice. The landlord and his family lived in the lower level.

One afternoon while I was out shopping at one of the big malls here, just as I was about to get into my car, my niece from Manitoba phoned. She had lots of news and it was so good to hear from her. Her daughter is three years old and the apple of my eye. Well, I broke down right there in the parking lot, sobbing away. I had to sit in my car for a while to pull myself together before driving home. I had been holding up fairly well till that point, trying not to miss people back home too much, just shedding a few tears and sniffles after phone calls. But the mall incident was major. You can only keep it in so long, I guess.

The bride veiled in cash, and the groom.

About marriage, and a wedding

The relationships between men and women in Arab countries, and their roles in Islamic culture, remain confusing and sometimes difficult topics for me. I can only convey what I observe here.

First of all, the men are allowed four wives. Whether a man actually has four wives or not seems to vary a lot from country to country, and in my opinion, is likely tied in with his financial position.

Among the younger generations of Omanis, one wife is accepted practice now. Few of the men I meet here have more than one wife. However, the men do banter jokingly about acquiring more wives, especially as they start taking on higher positions of authority and responsibility and make more money. When the wives hear such talk, they fail to see the humour in it. Their reactions indicate great displeasure at the idea of their status in the marriage being usurped. I am told that in Saudi Arabia most of the men have the allocated four wives, but I don't know this for a fact.

In Oman, if a gentleman takes a second wife, it is very important that he treat the two women, and their children, equally. One man I know here has two wives, living 250 km apart. He owns two homes, one for the wife in each city. He has to spend an equal amount of time with each family. This gentleman drives those 250 km every day to be with one of his families. He alternates weekends to be fair. Sounds a bit like a North American joint custody arrangement, except in this case, it's the wife who has joint custody of the husband. What a huge commitment of time and energy!

While at lunch one day with that particular gentleman and two of his co-workers, I was asked what I thought of this arrangement. My reply: "It would be way too much work to have two husbands!" This caused some confusion, as I was told I could not have two husbands. The idea created too great a leap in thinking for them.

15

My co-worker shared with me a story about a man who began with one wife. After a while, she became grumpy and hard to live with. This gentleman was concerned about the situation and came up with a great solution: he took a second wife. The first wife's mood immediately improved.

I tried very hard to see the humour in that little parable, but I'll admit it was a challenge.

Among the wealthy families here, the men do have multiple wives. I was at the Volvo dealership picking up the plates for my new car. A gentleman was seated in the salesperson's office. He had just purchased a new vehicle. I made a joke about how well the salesperson was doing, how he would soon be able to afford a new house. The other gentleman looked at me with a serious expression on his face and said arrogantly, "He should get another wife now, he has enough money. You know we can do that here."

I have mixed feelings about that aspect of Arab life. But I am only a visitor, and I try to remain an impartial observer.

The old, traditional process of marriage here is unlike the North American experience as well. The agreement is settled between the two families, with an adequate amount of money being given by the groom to the prospective wife's family. The couple meet, and if they seem compatible, the arrangements proceed. An Islamic holy man visits the prospective bride to see if she has accepted the man as her husband. If she agrees, the holy man proceeds to the prospective groom's home and the marriage takes place, without the prospective bride being present. The groom's male friends and family are there to help him celebrate his marriage.

The groom is responsible for all costs incurred at this event. He is also responsible for the bride's expenses. She must purchase a complete new wardrobe, since when she moves to his home she cannot, according to tradition, bring anything from her parents' home. The groom provides the new house and furnishings. The groom's family then proceeds to the bride's family home, without the groom; he stays behind at his home waiting for them to return. Dinner is served for the two families in celebration. The groom covers this cost. The next day the groom's family, the bride's family, and the bride all go to the groom's home, where he is waiting to welcome them. Another dinner celebration is had by all, which the groom again pays for. Then the families leave and the bride and groom begin their married life together. Sometimes there is a honeymoon, a new tradition being taken on by the younger generation, but it is not required or expected. It is important to note here that, until the wife arrives at her new home, the couple really have very little to do with each other, speaking on the phone a few times to discuss details, perhaps.

In June, a few months after I'd arrived, I was speaking with one of my clients, who had been married in April. His wife would be coming to live with him in July. They saw each other occasionally, and he allowed her to be part of the furniture-buying process. He was clear that this is tradition in his part of Oman, and that traditions vary from region to region.

My cohorts and I were puzzled when we first noticed that the stores were filled mostly with men. We soon discovered that shopping is usually done by the males, not the females. This is true of attendance at restaurants and coffee shops also. The men meet for dinner or coffee, but do not take their wives with them. I often wonder what the women are doing when the men are out. If the women want to go out shopping, it is not considered respectable for them to go alone, so you always see them in groups, especially in the malls.

There is a large community of expats in Oman who work in the labour and service industries. They represent various cultures, but the majority are from India and surrounding countries. Most of these expats are men who are here by themselves, leaving their wives and families at home. They make very little money, yet are able to live cheaply, usually six or eight sharing an apartment. They send whatever money they can to their families.

When in public, or if a man other than their husband, father, brother or son enters their homes, the women in Muscat wear long black robes called *abayas* over their clothing, and black scarves called *sheylas* covering their heads. The cuffs of the abayas and corners of the sheylas are often decorated with shiny colourful sequins – in other words, bling. Discreet bling, but bling nonetheless. A woman is a woman everywhere, I suppose. Arab men wear white, grey, beige, or brown full-length tunics and either a cap or a headscarf.

There is an expected dress code here for female expats. Shoulders and knees must be covered. No law requires that, but we respect the culture. I observe the dress code and cover my shoulders and knees, but I am still quite a bit more exposed than Arabic women. Quite risqué! I get stared at a lot. It doesn't bother me any more. When I first arrived I was really uncomfortable and felt like an alien. I later realize that many men here are living without their families and have little contact with women. The sight of western women in western wear is a feast for their eyes, perhaps. "Get over it!" became my unvoiced slogan.

Before I went to the Middle East, several people told me to be careful of the Arabian men. My initial thoughts were that I should be afraid of them, that they might harm me. But that's not it at all. The Arabian men are simply so very charming. They continuously compliment you. They are respectful, and yet playful. The flattery could easily go to your head and give you a big ego.

One time when I went to Dubai for the day, I hired a car and driver to tour me around, a good solution, since it isn't acceptable for a woman to travel alone. I spent the day with a charming Arabian man who was a very good tour guide. I was a bit giddy by the end of the day. He was absolutely taken with my red hair! He took me to an art gallery where I had a private tour provided by a gentleman who was also fascinated with my red hair. The men in Dubai are a little more forward than the men I had met in Oman, and were not shy in letting me know how attractive my hair was. It was a good thing my flight was leaving early.

So between those seductive Arabian nights and the charming Arabian men, coming to Oman turned out to be not such a bad choice…

Jackey and I were thrilled to attend a traditional Omani wedding ceremony, a rare occasion today, as most weddings are now held in hotels. One of Jackey's clients, Fatma, invited us. What a great honour! The ceremony was held at Amal's home. Amal was a friend of Fatma's, and Jackey and I knew her from her work administering our programs. Amal's home was a farm about fifty minutes outside Muscat. Her brother-in-law was the one getting married. Jackey and I did not know the bride.

The evening began with us arriving at Fatma's home. She was dressed in the traditional clothing of the southern part of Oman – Salalah – elegantly draped in layers of light green chiffon and silk, adorned with sequins and beads. The outfit reminded me of cool summer breezes. The traditional gold jewellery she wore was the perfect compliment to her dress.

Her husband, Harib, drove us out to the farm. Fatma's daughter, Arwa, age six, was with us. We arrived at a villa, one of many on this farm property. Several families live there, much like Canadian prairie farms, where two or three homes are built on the same property. We drove into the compound and were immediately greeting by the festive decorations in the yard. The concrete wall, which surrounds all homes here, was decorated with green material on the bottom, red on the top, and a border of white. The palm trees were bedecked with green lights, and the villa was festooned with strings of lights in red, orange, and white. There was a band setting up outside in the courtyard, which was strewn with bamboo mats for the guests to sit on. You could feel the excitement in the air immediately!

We went into Amal's villa around 9:00. She was still preparing for the celebration. We waited in one of the sitting rooms for her. One of the guests came around with an incense burner and we were invited to smudge our clothing with the aromatic incense. The children were running around, dressed in their best for the ceremonies. Then more guests started to arrive. Fatma explained that each woman was wearing the traditional clothing of her region. The women were stunning, and their clothing was breathtaking – exquisite silks, vivid colours, intricate beadwork, and lots of gold and silver jewellery. Feet and hands were decorated with henna tattoos in various designs and colours. I was in awe!

The sound of the band starting up drifted into the room. We went out on the balcony to watch. The band consisted of bagpipes and drummers, and many singers and dancers. It was an unexpected treat to hear the bagpipes; who would have thought…?

Our host Amal emerged in Omani garb traditional to the Muscat region: a tunic and pants, layers of gold, silver, and coral, intricate beadwork, pearls, and sequins. She wore a headband of pure gold filigree. Breathtaking! She led us outside to the courtyard where we were seated on the women's side. The men and women do not mix. Again, the sights, sounds, and smells were mesmerizing. Words cannot explain the feeling of elation and excitement I was feeling.

It was interesting to note that, although I was a foreigner at this event, I did not feel like one. I felt very comfortable and was having a great time. I spoke with many of the women there – a simple conversation, usually, since many of them knew only rudimentary English. Their wonderful smiles said it all, though. No words were necessary.

A light meal was served: tasty sandwiches, samosas, and small sponge cakes, followed by water and juices. Jackey and I had not eaten supper, so we were pretty hungry. (Jackey commented the next morning on how good a cheese sandwich can taste when you're starved.)

Then the excitement really began. All the women rushed into the villa, yelling what I can only describe as a coyote call, the correct word being *ululating*. The band members and men gathered outside the front door and one of the men began singing a song in Arabic through a bullhorn. This was to call the groom out of the house. One of the ladies in the band balanced a decorative container, the henna pot, on her head the whole time. She must have balanced that container on her head for at least thirty minutes. Then the groom emerged from the house in a white *dishdasha* (floor-length tunic), a traditional Omani *muzzar* (turban), and a sword and an Omani knife (*khanjar*) strapped to his waist with a scarf. He had a bright green silk scarf over his head, also adorned with multi-coloured beadwork. The ululating increased, the music intensified, and the groom was escorted to his car. So far, there has been no sign of the bride.

From here, everyone drove to the bride's parents' home in a convoy of buses and cars, emergency lights flashing the whole time. It was an exciting parade through the small village. Jackey and I were with Amal, Fatma, and three other women. Amal drove through narrow lanes and streets with her baby in one arm helping her steer, and her cell phone in the other hand. We arrived safely and happily. The father of the bride stood guard at the gates, as the men are not allowed to enter. In the courtyard, the female friends and relatives of the bride were gathered, and the bride was seated, completely covered, waiting for the groom. The groom joined her on a stage and the ladies present individually offered their well wishes and congratulations to the couple.

Then, much to our amazement, the wedding guests swathed the bride in paper money until she completely disappeared. Women went up and offered their congratulations.

The entire event was beautiful and I watched with anticipation as each moment unfolded. Eventually we were escorted back to our vehicles and driven back to Amal's villa. The henna container, minus the henna, was placed in front of the groom's chair in the courtyard. The musicians resumed playing and dancing. The festivities continued. By midnight, we were all very tired. Harib returned to pick us up, and we drove back to Muscat, leaving a very special world behind. I felt so privileged to have been part of that experience.

" Camel crossing" – my favorite road sign.

Red tape and driving

Driving in Oman is a wild and woolly adventure. To say you need to be alert is an understatement. A woman I know here – a fellow Canadian – won't allow her three children to utter one word in the car while she's driving. "This is no time for idle chatter," she'd tell them. "All my attention will be used up by the road."

So true. Not only is there a great deal of traffic, with cars coming from all directions, using up every inch of the highway, but lights, stop signs, and road signs are all mere decoration in Oman. For example, when you approach an intersection controlled by a stop sign, that simply means slow down, then start to nose into oncoming traffic; someone will let you in eventually. A single turning lane quickly becomes three lanes of vehicles trying to merge into the oncoming traffic. There are few signal lights, mostly roundabouts. The rule there is, just nose in; someone will stop and let you in rather than hit you, and if they don't let you in, then it's required that you honk your horn furiously. The turning lane is any of the four driving lanes. Driving on the wrong side of the road is common.

I cannot begin to describe the chaos that reigns during rush hours. Yet, there is an order here, too. If you want to change lanes, simply put on your turn signal and wait to be allowed in, no matter how backed up the traffic is. It never ceases to astound me that the system works.

Traffic lights are interesting: a red light turns orange before it turns green; as soon as it turns orange, everybody takes off. If you don't move fast enough, you'll soon know – the horns will start to blare behind you. I learned to ignore the horn-honking, since it's continuous and you're never quite sure who is honking at whom. The taxi drivers honk their horns on a regular basis whether it's needed or not. If they see someone walking down the street, they immediately pull into the curb lane, stopping all the traffic behind them, and start honking at the pedestrians to come to their taxi. They stop anywhere, even in the middle of a turning lane leading onto a major road or entrance ramp or roundabout.

And drivers often just back up onto busy streets without looking, so you have to be prepared to stop suddenly. If there is a bit of a traffic jam, drivers will move into the curb lanes, then right *onto* the curbs, and honk continuously. After all, if you honk your horn enough, eventually the traffic will get out of your way, right?

Manoeuvering on the streets can be nerve-wracking or it can be hilarious. Sometimes you want to gnash your teeth and tear out your hair, and other times the only sensible thing to do is laugh hysterically.

The highways are the same. The speed limit is 120 kph. It never fails that, when you pull into the passing lane to overtake a slower vehicle, a car will instantly appear on your tail, honking at you to get out of the way. Speed limits are not taken seriously here, even though cars are programmed to start beeping a warning just before you hit 120. When I first arrived I thought that was a great feature to have in vehicles. Once I'd been driving for a while, I found it just plain annoying.

In the city, you see men in orange coveralls wielding brooms and dustpans. Sometimes you see them using large palm branches. No mechanized street sweepers here – those men are the street cleaners.

Construction along the sides of the roads is vaguely marked by small, handwritten signs posted on the sidewalk that usually say, simply, "Men at Work." The highway workers have no hard hats, no boots, no safety vests. The lane of traffic where they are working is not blocked off.

Pedestrians are scary, too, here in Oman. Because of the absence of traffic lights, pedestrians cross the roads anywhere and everywhere. They have few crosswalks to keep them safe. On the major highway running through Muscat there is a pedestrian overpass only every five, maybe ten km. So pedestrians are dashing across the road, amongst the cars and trucks travelling at 120 kph. It happens on the highways as well. Lots of small towns mean lots of pedestrians running onto the highway. Man, you really need to keep your eyes open!

Muscat is sixty km long and five km wide. There are no maps of the city and people do not use street names or numbers. Asking for directions results in a gesture and, "Go that way for a few kilometres." Mosques are great landmarks here and they are pleasing to look at. The best piece of driving advice I got when I first arrived? Yacine, who is my employer Mohammed's brother and was our host for a few days, said, "If you get lost, don't worry, just find Sultan Qaboos Street and you will be okay." He was absolutely right – Sultan Qaboos Street is the main artery dissecting this long, narrow city. Once you know your way around a bit, driving is much easier. In fact, I learned to chuckle at the atrocities on the road. Every day was an adventure in keeping out of harm's way and musing over other drivers' near accidents.

When I arrived in Muscat on April 15th, 2008, I had to purchase a visitor's visa, good for sixty days with a thirty-day renewal requirement. The outstanding question in my mind during that time was: could I work legally in Oman with a visitor's visa? I'd heard that the Omani government was currently on a campaign of arresting people here without the correct visas. Yikes! I spoke with one of my neighbours, and she said her maid had been arrested and was in jail. The maid had a visa for residential work, but was also working at a hotel. Terror struck my heart! My co-worker Jackey was working at one of the Ministries. An arrest could have been embarrassing for them. One of the workers there told Jackey not to worry – they don't put Westerners in jail, they put us in hotel rooms. Somehow that didn't make me feel any better. Our sponsor told us, if the police ever came to arrest us, just tell them to call him. That really didn't make me feel any better, either. He assured us the residence cards and work visas would be approved shortly, they just needed His Excellency's signature. (Wasn't sure who His Excellency was at that point, but I didn't ask).

Once I'd been driving in Oman for about a month, I felt ready for a road trip, and decided I'd better drive to the nearest customs office to renew my visitor's visa. Sounded simple enough – take a day to drive to the customs office, which was at the United Arab Emirates border, renew the visa, and return. I chose a Thursday, the first day of the Omani weekend, even though I would have much rather spent the day relaxing after a busy week. But the visa was due to expire on Thursday, so I decided to make the best of it. Perhaps I could explore along the way to make the task more enjoyable. I soon discovered that navigating red tape in Arab countries is almost as chaotic as navigating its unruly highways.

Jackey came with me for the ride and to lend support. It was a three-hour drive. We decided not to go all the way to Dubai – all I had to do to renew my visa was cross the border – but rather to visit that fascinating city another time when we had a day or two. Today, the mission was renewing the visa and returning home at a decent hour. Sohar, a seaside town, was on the way; we were hoping to stop for lunch, and perhaps find some interesting shops along the way. Unfortunately, we arrived in Sohar at 1:30 PM, and in Omani tradition, everything was closed for the afternoon break, from 1:30 until 4:00 or so. Lunch was not going to happen, so we continued on, enjoying the farms and goats and camels. Farmers were parked along the roadside selling watermelons, muskmelons, and tomatoes. They even had scales sitting beside their trucks to weigh the produce. We did not stop, as we felt the urgency of getting the visa renewed. We decided to take a more leisurely pace on our way back. That was a brilliant decision, as it turned out, and we arrived at the Oman customs in good time.

The saga began. We pulled up to the border crossing on a divided highway. Our first stop was a small building with a friendly, helpful man working inside. He informed us that an exit ticket was required to leave the country. It cost two Omani rials (about $5). I told him I came to renew my tourist visa. He told us to continue on and stop at a building several meters up, then go three km down the road to a turn-around, come back, and report to the other side of the customs office, where we could complete our business. Or that's what we understood.

At that next building there was a line-up of cars, so I pulled in and we waited patiently. I noticed, however, that all the other traffic crossing the border just breezed past this line-up. The one and only English sign we saw in the area proclaimed, "Get Your Receipts at the Window." Deciding I didn't need a receipt for my exit ticket if no one else did, I motored on.

We drove for fifteen minutes. Suddenly we found ourselves at the UAE border crossing. What a shambles it was, considering that the country is the richest and fastest developing in the world! The customs office consisted of a group of trailers parked in the mountains. Travellers had to wait in line-ups outside in scorching temperatures. (Later I discovered this was a hastily assembled border station. Previously, there was no border crossing into the UAE – you came and went as you pleased.) Again, there were no signs, so we had to guess how to proceed. Not too many people spoke English. We lined up at a trailer. The line was blessedly short.

When we got to the front of the line the guard said, "Back, back." (He spoke no English, except for "Back, back".)

We were not sure what he meant. Finally a kind fellow in the line-up told us we needed to go to the other side of the trailer, the *back* of the trailer.

When we got there, we could clearly tell that it was the area for expatriates. We'd been waiting in the line reserved for Nationals. Soon another non-English-speaking guard approached us and said in an admonishing tone, "No exit stamp, no exit stamp."

Exit stamp? Again, we did not know how to interpret his cryptic message. But it was clear that he was not going to let us through. And again, a kind Omani gentleman directed us to an area where we could find the highway lane that would return us to the Oman customs building for our exit stamp. Back we went, scratching our heads in bewilderment, but at the same time marvelling at the intriguing, mountainous landscape. The fact that photos are not allowed to be taken between border crossings, however, had been clearly conveyed, despite the dearth of proper signage regarding other procedures.

Before reaching the Oman customs we had to stop at a checkpoint where a guard looked in the trunk; this was the first place any kind of search was carried out. He gave me a ticket and off we went to the Oman border. This time we stopped at a different customs building. A friendly Omani guard told us we needn't have come all the way to the border to renew the tourist visa, we could have gone to the airport in Muscat. *Aargh!* But since we were already here, we decided to continue on with the process.

We were instructed to return to the window where we'd purchased the first exit ticket. There we paid another two rials for a new one. The same official served us. He took our money and enjoyed a hearty laugh at our expense.

We proceeded to the window which we had originally thought dispensed receipts, and were extremely relieved to find that was indeed the place to acquire the coveted the exit *stamp*.

Jackey and I began to feel pretty good about our success. Thinking we were done, we turned around, our destination the immigration office at the Oman border. We did, however, have to endure the trunk search once more. We arrived at the Oman immigration office to renew the Visa, proudly brandishing our exit stamps and our trunk-check stamp.

Surprise, surprise, those two documents did not satisfy the customs officials. We needed *entry and exit stamps* from the *UAE* customs; we had only the Oman *exit stamps*.

Oh yeah – whoops!

After a refreshing cup of tea in a café in the comfortable, modern, air-conditioned Oman immigration building, we set out again. For the third time, the exit ticket guy saw our lovely but by now exasperated faces appearing at his window, and again, the laughter. We told him the whole sad tale, and out of sympathy, he allowed us through without paying another two rials.

We bypassed the Oman exit stamp building this time, as we already had that. We got our entrance stamp to the UAE at the same dismal trailer where we'd been rejected on our first trip. We drove up the road and turned around to return to the exit side of the UAE border crossing. As we approached the border crossing one more time, we were again unsure which building dispensed the exit stamp. We were half-way there, had our Oman exit stamp, and our UAE entrance stamp. Perseverance! As we entered the customs area, we spotted a sign advising that trucks stay left and cars stay right. Being good Canadians, we followed the signs. By being good Canadians, I mean that generally Canadians are well behaved and follow signs and rules. They are orderly in line-ups, making sure everyone has their rightful turn.

As we passed by yet another dilapidated trailer we saw people lined up outside. I hit the brakes and found a place to park on the side of the road. Reasoning that it's better to be safe than sorry, we went into the trailer, just to check. Hooray! This was, in fact, the UAE exit stamp building. We joined a short line-up and were feeling pretty good again, hoping we would soon be done.

Not so. The gentleman in front of us had encountered a slight problem involving his very pregnant wife and a lapsed tourist visa. Our guard took him to another window and we were left standing in line for fifty minutes before he returned.

Several busloads of people had since arrived and there was a huge backlog of travellers. Many of them, seeing the gentleman with the visa problem as the only one at that wicket, started to line up behind him. As you can imagine, there was a near riot when the guard finished with the gentleman and returned to his original post. It took only another ten minutes for Jackey and me to get our exit stamps. By the time we left, people were pushing and shoving, cutting in, muttering threats.

We made our third and final stop at the trunk checkpoint. The guards there did not speak English, so they asked no questions, just sent us quizzical looks. We were too frustrated and tired to take any offence.

Back at the Oman immigration building, we met several people who had been stuck at the UAE customs with us, and we were all very happy to share our misery and our relief.

A mere three hours had passed since we'd begun our red tape run-around. We spent more time driving back and forth between border crossings then we did getting there!

We were hungry and tired by the time we reached Sohar at 7:00. Deliriously happy to find all shops and cafés open, we stopped for a rest and a bite to eat. The whole ordeal taught us useful lessons in being patient when it comes to navigating the pandemonium of Arab bureaucracy. And about giving yourself lots of time.

(Footnote: When you purchase a new vehicle in Oman, the dealer puts a green license plate on your car. This allows you to drive until your permanent yellow plate is ready. About two weeks after my fun-filled experience renewing my visa, I went to the car dealer to pick up my yellow plate and I commented on how long I had driven with the green plate. The salesman's response was: no worries, you can drive for a year on the green plate as long as you don't leave the country. But I had left the country with green plates. Good thing I didn't know the rules then. Apparently, none of the border guards did, either. Life is just one adventure after another…)

My Omani friends.

My new Omani friends

Among my early, more memorable social activities was an outing with Ali, who was one of the participants in the Results Centred Leadership program. One Wednesday he invited me to spend the next day with him and his family. (I found it tough to get used to Thursdays and Fridays being the weekend.) He was planning an excursion into the countryside. I had some reservations about accepting the invitation, since he has two wives. We would be accompanied by only one spouse, Wife #1. I was a little shaky on the politics of the whole deal, but I didn't feel I could pass up the opportunity.

I met the family at 9:15 the next morning, at a pre-determined location, one of the shopping malls. First, I was introduced to his wife Yasmine, then their three daughters, Safia, twelve; Samar, ten; and five year-old Ayisha. All spoke English except the youngest daughter. The maid, an Indonesian who also did not speak English, accompanied us. She had been with the family for seven years and had learned Arabic. After a stop at a service station for water, juice, and snacks to add to our cooler full of food, we were off. Our first destination: Al Hoota cave.

We drove through Nizwa and past the old fort. There wasn't time to stop at the fort that day. We arrived early, thanks to Ali's driving skills, if you can call driving at speeds of 180–200 kph skillful. I tried to take comfort in the fact that we were travelling in a solid Cadillac Escalade. In Oman, seat belts are required in the front seats, but not the back. I found it somewhat unnerving, bouncing around in my seat as we took sharp turns or made sudden stops. I yearned for the security of a seat belt holding me in place.

Ali had reserved a spot for us on the tour, as Thursdays are very busy at the cave. We arrived around 11:00. The tour took about an hour-and-a-half in total. Al Hoota was breathtaking – cave formations, stalactites, stalagmites, and columns which have evolved over millions of years. Lots of colour –

pinks, yellows, golds, and greys. There are two lakes in Al Hoota cave, filled with fresh water from desert rains. The freshwater lakes are home to a unique species of fish, called blindfish (*Garra barreimiae*). They have no eyes, but have long barbels for sensing food. Their bodies lack pigment as a result of living in little or no light. Al Hoota cave houses very small bats, which we saw only in pictures. They sleep during the day inside the cave. A new species of spider was discovered there, the Hoota hunting spider. It is a very large spider. We didn't see any live specimens of those, either, thank goodness. I was in awe of the people who first discovered and explored the cave without electric lights to guide them, and without the assistance of protective railings along the walkways and steps properly carved into the rock.

The tour included a visit to the cave museum. I was pleased to find an exhibit illustrating the geological history of the mountains. Since my arrival in Muscat, I had been mesmerized by the mountains, rock formations in all the colours of the rainbow with different layers weaving patterns throughout. In the museum I discovered that those unique mountains were formed by three Ice Ages. The cave tour turned out to be an intriguing trek through history.

We decided to delay eating until we got up into the mountains. We began our ascent. Jebel Shams (Sun Mountain), is the highest mountain in Arabia. Part of the road was paved, but a good portion of it was really rough. Again, I was grateful for Ali's skills as a driver and the Caddy as our vehicle.

Our first stop in the mountains was a stunning lookout point. Across the road there were sheltered picnic tables. Within a few minutes of our arrival, vendors emerged from a hut built into the side of the mountain, hoping to sell their wares. But they did not detract from the beauty of the scenery.

Our next stop: the family's favourite destination. Ali has permission from a family who owns some property in the mountains to use it for picnics. The maid began preparations, and in a few minutes, she'd laid out a large mat covered with an abundance of food and beverages. The temperatures were cooler up there – only 28oC. It was a nice break from the heat. Soon enough the goats got wind of us and started moving in. The youngest daughter is afraid of goats and her screams echoed off the mountain sides until the parents were able to calm her down.

Lounging around the picnic site was a treat. It was the first occasion I'd had to spend time with a family since I'd left Canada. I enjoyed observing the displays of affection and the easy conversations in Ali's family. My earlier misgivings melted away. I felt blessed to be there, and I thought, six months ago – heck, *three* months ago – I never would have believed this would be my life today.

Our relaxing and eating done, we proceeded down the mountain. The road down was like a roller coaster ride – up, down, and around. Samar, the middle daughter, succumbed to motion sickness. She became very quiet and very pale. I had sympathy for her. Before heading up the mountain, her mother had warned the children that they should not eat at the picnic because they would get sick on the way down. Her prophesy came true – partly, anyway. Luckily, we'd made it almost all the way down the mountain before the mini-disaster struck poor Samar.

We stopped for the family to attend prayers at a small temple in a rural village, then headed off to Nizwa for dinner. Curiously enough, and against Ali's wishes, we went to a Pizza Hut. The daughters had voted and the decision was unanimous. Samar had by then fully recovered. What a bizarre sequence of events, though: al Hoota cave, a sojourn on an idyllic mountain side, prayers in a village temple, then dinner at Pizza Hut!

And we weren't done yet. In Nizwa, we explored the *souq* (marketplace). Here shops sold local crafts such as pottery, silver, jewelled ornaments, and carpets. As well, we visited the souq's fruit-and-vegetable stands. Ali bought Omani bananas for us to nibble on as we drove home – tiny, tasty bananas.

I arrived home tired, but still high on the experiences the day had provided.

Residence card blues

Once Talal had our final residence card papers in his hand, Jackey and I needed to go for a medical, *i.e.*, blood tests and fingerprints. When that was completed, supposedly all that was left would be to go to the immigration office to pick up the residence card. Talal thought we could get it all done in one day. Sounded simple, but I should have realized that nothing is simple when it comes to Omani bureaucracy. As much as things are different, they are the same: bureaucracy, bureaucracy, bureaucracy!

Jackey and I re-scheduled our appointments that Saturday so we could go for the medical and fingerprints. We arrived at Talal's office just before noon so that he could drive us. Faisal, a part time associate of Talal's, came along because we needed to have an Omani person with us. (Talal is Jordanian.) We drove to a part of Muscat called Ruwi; it is the financial district, an older area of the city. We noticed some different and interesting architecture there. We entered a back alley and Talal announced, "You are now entering one of the worst areas in Muscat." Yikes.

He led us into a very old and shabby Government office. What a shock! Not the shabbiness of the offices; we saw about four hundred men waiting in a line that snaked up and down the stairs through the building. The stench of all that humanity crowded into a small space was overwhelming. Jackey and I both had to work at keeping our stomachs calm. The men were waiting to get forms for the blood test. All I could think was: *Oh my God*. I could not even begin to imagine standing in that line-up. I didn't want to think about how many hours the men had already been waiting.

To our immense relief, we were ushered to a separate queue for women. No one was in that line-up. At the same time as I rebelled mentally against such gender discrimination, I was grateful for the ladies' queue. We got our forms quickly enough and Talal led us upstairs to the correct clinic. In the waiting room, about thirty women were ahead of us. The two male guards who generally kept order and called the numbers for admittance to the room for the blood tests were obviously out of patience. Every time they entered the waiting room, the women would press around them, chattering away. No other men were allowed in the room and most of the women did not speak Arabic or English. The result was minor mayhem. The guards shouted and ordered everyone to sit down. Peace was temporarily restored. Then they came around to check the ladies' numbers. The guards seemed to be quite abrupt and rude, but considering the language barriers they faced, they did pretty well. Eventually they noticed Jackey and me and moved us up the queue. Again, it was with mixed feelings that Jackey and I accepted the preferential treatment.

It took only an hour-and-a-half after that to get the blood tests finished, which was long enough. Then we texted Talal to let him know we were finished, and he met us out in the hallway. We noticed that all the women who'd been in line were met by male companions outside. Many of the women were housemaids, very young, coming from other countries by themselves and unable to speak the language.

It was quite an eye-opening experience. It made me feel extremely grateful to be born in Canada and to enjoy all the privileges of being a Canadian citizen. In my home country, I took it for granted that I would acquire employment, and that I would make a salary that allowed me to live comfortably. Suddenly, all that seemed so easy – no visa required, no language barriers, no cultural barriers. Canada is certainly a land of luxuries for its citizens. It occurred to me how often I and others take it all for granted. Living in Oman gave me a new appreciation for Canada.

Before Jackey and I could be fingerprinted, Talal and Faisal had to take a form to another government office, still in Ruwi, and get it stamped. They dropped off the form and were told it would be half-an-hour. Talal laughed to himself – half-an-hour! Half-in-hour in an Oman government office is an oxymoron. We went for lunch and then checked back. Not ready. Talal drove us back to our cars and Faisal stayed to collect the form. I called Talal later on his cell. 6:30 PM and he and Faisal were just leaving the office with the stamped papers.

The fingerprint office was closed by then; we made arrangements for the next morning. Fortunately, the fingerprint office opened at 7:30, and neither Jackey nor I was meeting with clients until a little later. The office was in the same area of Muscat After I'd lived in Oman for about three months, I experienced a short period of what I call The Blues, a time of feeling lonesome and sad, of missing everyone back in Canada and not being truly connected to life in Oman. At the same time, I could say with confidence that I quite liked my life in Oman. Such a beautiful country!

Part of the problem was a crisis that arose involving my residence card, causing a great deal of frustration to surface. I'd been in Oman since April 17th and had been repeatedly assured that my residence card would take only a few weeks to be processed. By the middle of June, it was still not done. After some investigation, I received the good news that all the papers had been signed by the Minister of Immigration and were in the sponsor's hands; only a few details needed to be cleared up. Perhaps the waiting and frustrations were nearly over after all. But I had been saying that for close to three months and I remained just a tad sceptical.

Much later, I found out that problems arose because we were establishing a new company in Oman, and there were several unforeseen regulations that needed to be met. Talal was our liaison with our sponsor, and he worked hard to get this done as fast as possible. But often things such as government rules and partnership agreements were out of his hands.

The main issue with not possessing an official residence card was that I couldn't open a bank account or acquire a credit card without one. When I left Canada I closed my accounts and cancelled my credit cards on the assumption that the residence card would take only a couple of weeks. In the meantime, my employer had been paying me in cash. Then in June he left the country for a while, not worrying about my situation because he was certain the residence card was on its way to me and he could simply transfer money to my bank account. It didn't happen. Nevertheless, I expected to receive my salary in some form or other on July 1st (Canada Day – yay!), and spent accordingly.

July 1st came and went, finding me with an almost empty wallet and no word from my employer. I began to panic. Without access to funds I was feeling pretty stuck.

I called Talal on the off chance that arrangements had been made and he'd just forgotten to call me. Of course, that wasn't the case. After exchanging a few emails with my employer, I finally received some cash three days later. It was fortunate that Talal had lent me some money while I waited. Eventually I began to think of him as the Magic Man, since he was always able to help me, no matter what the problem. He was a lifesaver.

But I had started to panic. I didn't know anyone to call; my employer and my co-worker Jackey were both out of the country. It took quite a bit of self-talk to get settled down. That was the first time since arriving in Oman that I actually thought of leaving, of returning to the familiarity and comfort of my home in Canada.

To add to my frustration level, I had been hoping to book airline tickets. The plan was that I would go back to Canada at the end of July, for a visit and to coordinate travel plans with my son in Saskatoon, Saskatchewan. We would meet in Toronto and return to Muscat together. So I began to search for a way to get airline tickets without a credit card. That, I found, was virtually impossible. The travel agent I visited wanted double the normal price for the tickets, so I decided it wise not to go that route. Then I found an airline with a ticket office nearby and booking agents that accepted cash for tickets. Their price was only $1,000 higher than anything I found online! As a last resort, I spoke to Talal about my problem of not being able to purchase airline tickets at the cheaper online rates, and he offered me the use of his credit card. Talal to the rescue once again. I paid him in cash and used his card.

Another time during this rather low period in my life in Oman, I received a cheque from the US, but couldn't cash it or deposit it without a bank account. I asked Talal if he could deposit the cheque and give me the cash when the cheque cleared. We made a trip to his bank and were told that the banks here do not accept foreign cheques. Even if I had an account they would not accept it. I'm not sure why – something to do with bank charters. The language barrier got in the way. Plus, I went into shock discovering that I could not receive cheques in Oman. Oh, the frustration!

I looked forward to the day when I could make an entry in my journal that said, "Hurray, hurray, hurray; I am now officially a resident of Oman for two years!" No more worrying about being arrested for working without a visa. No more worrying about how to survive without access to banking. Even with its limits, at least it's banking.

To illustrate the awkwardness of my position when I was card-less and therefore bank-less: Upon arrival in Oman I received a $20,000 advance to purchase a car and furniture. I had to carry that cash around with me. I kept it in a plastic bag in my purse. And when Jackey left the country for a week, she asked me to safeguard her money as well. At one time, I believe I was carrying about $38,000 on my person. Interesting how after a short period of time I just relaxed and was not overly concerned about the huge sum of money in my handbag.

Jackey's son was amazed at her wad of bills. He said, "You're just like a drug dealer carrying that bag of cash around!"

It's all a matter of perspective, isn't it?

that I worked in, called Quorm. Once more, we were escorted by Talal. The building was again dismal – old and poorly maintained. It was very clean, though. The fingerprint process went relatively smoothly, except that extra copies of some forms were required. Talal had to run out and get copies made. (We wondered how far he would have to go for this, but, being a smart and resourceful man, he simply went to the nearest police station and had the job done there.) At the fingerprint office there was again a segregated area for the women. The male companions had to stay behind a partition while the ladies were fingerprinted. We giggled as we watched the men peering at us over the partition, only their eyes and the tops of their heads visible. They were nervous about their charges (the ladies) being taken care of without their presence. Fortunately, none of us could get lost, as there was only one way in and one way out of that room. The process was completed by 8:15 AM. Success! We were getting close!

Off to work for the day. Jackey and I planned to meet Talal and Faisal at 4 PM at an agreed location. We then needed to head out to Seeb, which is at the extreme north end of Muscat. We were pretty excited, as we were starting to believe that we would actually get our cards that day. This time the office was new, modern, spacious, and sophisticated. The rows of chairs in the waiting room were neat and orderly, and the call numbers were posted electronically in various places so you could wait in queue comfortably. We were ushered into a private office where our photos were taken. Exposure to white Western women obviously flustered the young Arabian officer who was in charge there. Talal paid very close attention to make sure all the spellings on the forms were correct. Then, off to another part of the building to collect the cards.

The cards came out wrong, even after Talal's careful scrutiny. Jackey's information was with my picture, and my information was with hers! Jackey's was corrected in a fairly short period of time, and she hurried away to meet someone coming to her villa to install curtain rods. Talal, Faisal, and I stayed behind. It took a little attention but Talal eventually got everything straightened out, and in about fifteen minutes, it was complete. I had my residence card in my hand!

At last, the day of celebration had arrived. After three months, I finally received my two-year residence card for Oman, which was also my work visa. Hurray, hurray! I was ecstatic! It was all I could do to contain my pleasure. I felt like turning somersaults in the parking lot!

The day I received the card, I stopped caring about the delay. I'm still grateful to my sponsor, Talal, for his patience and persistence in getting the job done.

The very next day I went to the bank and opened an account. No more carrying wads of cash in my purse. I picked up an application form for a cell phone plan immediately. I was starting to feel human again.

One more task that we would have to tackle was getting the proper driver's license. This, too, was apparently very simple, just a matter of completing more forms, showing my Canadian license, and paying a fee of twenty Omani rials. Talal said he would work on the forms at once. I basked in the prospect of becoming a legitimate driver in Oman.

But at that point, I wanted only to focus on a different and more important project: my up-coming trip back to Canada.

Wendy, Dad, and me in Manitoba on Dad's eightieth birthday.

A visit home

Oh, the absolute joy of returning home for a visit! In August, I went back to Winnipeg, Canada for a break. It was so good to get away from the summer heat for a while. I'd had enough of 45o temperatures on an ongoing basis. In Winnipeg, everyone was complaining about the cool summer they were having. I was in heaven with temperatures of 25o–27oC during the day. A little cool at night, 10o–12o, but a sweater or a fleece easily chased away the chill. What a relief!

After several months in the desert, I found the greenery astounding. And it was so good to watch the cloud formations moving across the skies, some days quickly, some days slowly. In Muscat when it is overcast, everyone is very excited about the comfortable weather and they want to spend the day at the beach! The Canadian sunsets and sunrises were inspiring. Muscat rarely has cloud cover. The sunsets here, too, are pretty, but very different from sunsets on the Canadian prairies.

I stayed with Bob, my boyfriend at the time, and basked in his kindness during my stay. I was pleasantly surprised by how well he had taken care of the vegetable and flower gardens. They were stunning.

The first week, I got caught up on business that needed to be taken care of since my departure. It seemed like minor things – banking, insurance, drivers license, credit cards, Revenue Canada, credit balances on telephone and hydro accounts – but each took quite awhile. Of course, I spent time with family and friends. It was so wonderful to have people around that I knew and loved dearly. I was also pleasantly surprised by all the changes that had occurred since I'd left only three months ago. The families were growing and changing in many fabulous ways.

Then Bob and I were off on our yearly kayaking trip. We made base camp at Black Lake, Manitoba, and paddled the lakes and river systems in

Nypoming Park, one of Canada's national parks. We started our days with a hearty breakfast of bacon, eggs, and pancakes. Lunch was then packed for the day and we enjoyed that lunch along the shoreline. We returned early evening to heat up a satisfying pre-cooked meal. Bedtime followed quickly, as we were usually tired from our day of adventure. Heavenly. The weather was great – no rain except for one storm that occurred during the night. Most days were overcast, which meant great paddling and no need to stop and get out of the sun for a while. There was an abundance of wildlife on this trip. Our first day out we came across fifteen hawks circling back and forth on the air thermals. The birds were awe-inspiring. We stayed and watched for about fifteen minutes, during which we tried to get some pictures, but our camera was not sufficient for the task. Our third day out I came across three curious little otters. They played with me for about ten minutes. I felt very honoured as they chattered away and kept popping up a little closer to my boat each time. On one of our more adventuresome days we kayaked down a river system that emptied in and out of several lakes. This required several portages. At one of the falls, which I portaged while Bob ran the rapids, I was blessed with observing twelve butterflies feeding on a patch of wildflowers. I rested for a few minutes and enjoyed the gift.

The last week of my holiday I spent visiting friends and relatives. It was my father's eightieth birthday and we had a great celebration for him, thanks to my sister Wendy, who did all the organizing. I helped out a bit the day of the party, but felt very grateful for the preparatory work Wendy had done. About seventy-five people attended the afternoon event. Dad was pleased as punch. It was a tremendous day, all in all. I got to visit with many relatives I might not have had time to see otherwise.

Many people asked me: did Canada seem different? The answer is yes. One thing that was especially disturbing was the violence. There had been a tragic incident on a highway bus where a man had been beheaded by another one of the passengers, a brutal and inexplicable murder. The media assault that followed was horrific. The detail of the gruesome incident and eye – witness accounts were repeated over and over again. I found that shocking. Oman is such a gentle country and the people are so kind. I am not sure such a horrific incident would occur in their country. Crime is dealt with very differently in a country that is a dictatorship, although I do not know details and hope I never do. I understand crime is not tolerated and is dealt with severely. I do know that the kind of sensationalism and publicity that followed the incident in Canada would not occur in Oman. The crime would not be promoted to the public, it would be considered dishonourable and disgraceful, not something to brag about. The constant media barrage in Canada was terrible to me. I realized I did not notice it so much when I lived in Canada. In this case, I avoided it by not listening to the news or reading the newspaper. I very clearly realized that I did not miss this aspect of our culture at all.

The other difference was from a personal safety standpoint. There is not a place in Oman that I had been to where I felt threatened or at risk in any way. I remember an Omani gentleman telling me a story about New York City and how terrible it was that the residents could not go to many parts of the city without fearing for their lives, and how as a tourist he was very aware of those dangers. Returning to Canada made me realize how true that is of many areas of our cities. As a tourist, you just don't go there. Such is the case even in my little Winnipeg, a city the same size as Muscat.

It did seem funny to me that, there I was in the Middle East, an area of the world constantly being portrayed as an incredibly dangerous part of the world, and yet I felt safer there than I did in my own country. Oman is known throughout the GCC as a friendly and hospitable place. I can certainly attest to that.

On my way back to Oman I stopped for a visit with some dear Winnipeg friends who had moved to the countryside about an hour away from Toronto. My son Joey flew in from Saskatoon, I from Winnipeg. He and I met at the Toronto airport and spent the next few days enjoying the hospitality of Gai and Rob.

My son is twenty-eight years old and I'd brought him up as a single parent. We are very close. He was considering moving to Oman – wonderful for me and an excellent experience for him. So he returned to Oman with me to check things out. Joey was my first visitor in Muscat. It was interesting to see Muscat and Oman through his eyes, the eyes of a newcomer, bringing back many memories of my own arrival in this country. One of the things that struck me was how similar his and my reactions were to the landscape. It still strikes me as odd to see all the empty lots as barren expanses of sand. I vividly remember driving to Sohar, two-and-a-half hours north of Muscat one day, and seeing the children playing football (what we call soccer in Canada) in the fields. My immediate reaction was, oh, the poor children having to play in the barren sand; this was quickly followed by the realization that, of course the fields are sand! I don't respond that way to seeing Canadian children playing in dirt fields. In fact, I have fond memories of playing baseball and football (*Canadian* football) as a young girl in the park behind our house, and – yes – the field was dirt. Joey was taken aback, too, by all the sand everywhere.

I loved to see the beauty of this country reflected in his eyes and his thoughts. I remembered how overwhelming it was at first, but with time I had became accustomed to the beauty all around me.

My son had worked his way through university as a supervisor in a call centre, first in the area of cell phones, and then credit cards. That experience made him a good negotiator and a good judge of character. He'd heard it all! Once he'd tried bartering in the *souqs* here, he quickly became very good at it. The markets here all operate on the barter system. We went to Dubai one weekend and, of course, had to hit the souqs. Amazing places! Joey began the barter process with two gentlemen for a briefcase. They made their first offer, a very high price, 450 durhams. My son countered with 200 durhams. They said, "We sell these for 450 durhams to lots of people." My son's response was classic: "Who do you sell these to for 450 durhams? Nobody pays 450 durhams for this, just show me one person you have sold this to for that price."

The gentlemen were so impressed with his skills they started to laugh immediately. Then they got down to the real bartering process. The final deal was two briefcases for 175 durhams each. Ten durhams = one Omani rial, and one Omani rial = $2.60 USD. The transition was interesting for me, because in Dubai I did not translate durhams into dollars, but into Omani rials. Another note: we say Omani rials because other GCC countries' currencies are also called rials. In Saudi Arabia, though, it is spelled *riyal*.

I was worried about what Joey would eat, as I consider him to be a picky eater, but he really enjoyed the food here. In my opinion, the food in Oman is outstanding – it would be very difficult not to enjoy it. My sister was planning to come for a visit in February. She is also a picky eater, but I hoped she would be fine with the food, too.

The Muslims observed Ramadan in September. Ramadan is a month of fasting from sunrise to sunset, nothing to eat or drink. It is a month focused on compassion and understanding of those less fortunate than we may be, those who do not eat, not by choice but because of their economic position. It's a month of good deeds and contemplation on spiritual practices.

The beginning of the fast is Imsak. It is announced every morning around 4:30 AM by the first call to prayers for the day. The end of the fast is around sunset, or 6:30, every day. The exact times are published in the newspapers. The end of the fast is Iftar. The fast is usually broken with dates and tea, followed by prayers. The fast is also considered to be broken if you have nasty thoughts of other people and circumstances.

Some then have a big meal after that set of prayers. The next set of prayers is at 7:30 PM, and it's common for families to gather for the big meal of the day around 8:30 or 9. This meal is usually very elaborate, with many traditional Ramadan foods (kind of like turkey at Christmas or pumpkin pie at Thanksgiving). Most offices close for the day at 1 PM and many of the Omani people spend the afternoon resting. The normal 6 PM traffic congestion does not occur until 10:00 during Ramadan.

Stores and malls change their hours to stay open later and offer special

Ramadan pricing. Restaurants and hotels have Iftar buffets and special rates on rooms. It is a time of great celebration with family and friends. Food is traditionally exchanged. An Omani person told me jokingly that Ramadan is the best time to buy something – you can be assured you will not be taken advantage of!

The city is like a ghost town, only expats out and about. The restaurants and stores are deserted until 10 at night. Very strange; most interesting is the Omani people themselves. Many of them are very tired during this time due to the change in sleep patterns. But mostly I found them introspective and reflective. A quiet and gentle people become even more so during Ramadan.

It's considered extremely rude to eat or drink in public during Ramadan, so the restaurants are closed until evening. I really missed the tea boy bringing refreshment at break time on workdays.

Jackey's family finally arrived in Muscat in August. Over the ensuing months I spent a lot of time with the Backmans. It was so much fun! Eric was ten – an easy going playful young lad with a great sense of humour – and Jonathon fourteen, on his journey to manhood – easy to converse with and interested in the larger world; he was always full of queries about adult lifestyles – work, places in the world to live, music.

It is always interesting, experiencing this country through the eyes of our visitors, and I realized that I would have that pleasure many times as various friends and family members came to see me during my sojourn here.

My son Joey – his first visit.

43

Destinations

While Joey was visiting, our first destination was Al Sawadi Beach Resort, about one hour north of Muscat. It being August, the slow tourist season, the place wasn't too busy. Joey and I stayed at the resort for two nights for the price of one, a summer promotion. We arrived late in the afternoon and spent the rest of the daylight hours out on a Sea-Doo, Joey driving and me on the back. (They had only one Sea-Doo.) The hotel offered an excellent dinner buffet in the evening and we enjoyed the delicious food sitting out on one of the patios. Because we had booked snorkelling for 8:00 the next morning, we went to the room and off to sleep fairly early.

Our snorkelling excursion revealed a whole world alive and abundant under the water. We spent a full day exploring, seeing turtles, barracuda, eels, and a variety of colourful, exotic fish. Our guide caught up with us at one of the coral reefs. He spotted a turtle and grabbed our attention. He swam underwater for a long period of time (I was wondering how he could hold his breath that long) and caught up with the turtle. I was expecting the man to grab hold of it, but he did not, he simply swam beside it and patted its shell. Once again, I was in awe of the gentleness of the Omani people.

That underwater experience made me think about how much we miss every day, how we often focus on only one dimension of life. It took forty-five minutes to reach a private island for this snorkelling excursion, and I was totally unaware of life under the sea during that drive. On the way back, I pondered the question: how often am I just riding along, oblivious to life around me?

We returned to the resort mid-afternoon and were ready for a nap. Boy, were we ready for a nap! After conking out for a few hours, we both woke up realizing how exhausted we were. We ordered room service and had another great meal. Joey by that time was suffering from severe sunburn, even though he'd been diligent with the SPF30. Lesson learned. Both of us, however, thoroughly enjoyed the time at Al Sawadi.

The next weekend we ventured up to Dubai, a bustling city of four million people and constant construction. Because Dubai gets so much media coverage around the world, Joey was quite thrilled to be there. We behaved like the tourists we were. There is lots to see in Dubai and our two days there were jam-packed. The Dubai museum, for example, is a fantastic attraction. It's wonderful to see pictures of Dubai between 1930 and 1970, a small struggling desert village. Then oil was discovered and everything changed. The museum documents the history of current development in Dubai. There are excellent displays depicting life before development, from the perspectives of both the people and the land.

For the avid shopper, there are at least six malls in the city with 350 stores in each. The largest mall has 800 stores, and a new mall under construction will have 1200 stores. Yikes, that's scary! I am not a shopper. Joey and I did, however, have great fun bartering for our goods in open-air markets. Even though we were not there during high tourist season, the souqs were bustling with people and activity. We took a ride on the water taxis, wooden boats that cross Dubai creek, going from the Traditional Souq to the Gold Souq. It was an exhilarating couple of days. I so love the souqs and the bartering. In Muscat, there are also a Traditional and a Gold Souq. I have gotten to know several of the owners of shops and love going down to visit with them and barter. They are always happy to see faithful customers and they bring you tea or water. It feels so much more connected for me than shopping at an immaculately decorated store in a cold, unfriendly mall.

When Dawna, a friend from Winnipeg, arrived a month later, we again made the trip up to Dubai. This time we hired a driver and saw all the highlights in one day. We didn't spend as much time in the souqs, and I was introduced to a few new things I had not seen before. Our driver was very knowledgeable about Dubai; he was originally from Pakistan, but had lived in Dubai for seventeen years. He had a quick smile and a friendly manner, sharing lots of information about the Dubai of the past, the present Dubai, and future plans for the city. In the evening, we went on a *dhow* dinner cruise. (A dhow is a traditional wooden boat.) The meal was fabulous and we enjoyed the company of an interesting couple from the UK.

Joey, Dawna, and I spent a day on a sailboat as well. The boat typically holds thirty people, but due to the low tourist season we were lucky enough to be on it with about ten people. It was fabulous. We cruised out to an island in a different direction from our previous trip and spent the afternoon snorkelling. In addition to the abundant species of fish, we discovered an area of breathtaking purple coral. We even snorkelled into a cave, just for fun. It was a great way to spend a day. On the return trip to the mainland, the sunset was spectacular, providing a perfect end to our day of sailing.

Joey and Dawna, along with my co-worker Jackey's husband, Fred, spent a day on a desert safari without me. Jackey and I had to work that day. I must admit that, after continuous company for four weeks, I really enjoyed having my apartment to myself after work. The group went dune-bashing, swimming in a *wadi* (a stream at the bottom of a valley or gulley), and camel riding. They came home glowing and full of stories to share about their exciting day. I had yet to try those things, but planned to do so when more company arrived in November and December.

One afternoon, Fred, Dawna, and I drove out to Al Nahda Resort and Spa. It's situated in the desert, so our time was spent lazing around the pool and swimming. There are lots of different spa treatments available, so I planned to go back and try some of them another time. This was an afternoon of leisurely conversation, reading, and relaxing. Later that evening, Jackey and her two boys joined us and we all had dinner together. It was still Ramadan, so we had an *Iftar* (break the fast) buffet. We ate Omani style, sitting on cushions on the floor.

That same week, Dawna, Fred, his two boys, and I spent an afternoon at Al Sawadi Beach Resort. This time we had access to both the pool area and the sea. It was delightful. I treated myself to a wonderful Indian traditional ayurvedic massage. When I rejoined the group, they said I smelt like spicy Indian food! Ha, ha, ha. I didn't care; I was floating in bliss from the treatment.

Dawna and I spent a night in traditional straw huts at Green Turtle resort, about three hours south of Muscat, still in the Sultanate of Oman. I say "traditional" huts, tongue in cheek, because the huts were air-conditioned. The temperature went down to 24oC that night and we were on the sea with a cool breeze, so we didn't need the air-conditioning. We drove down to the resort along the Coast Highway, which is not open to the public officially, but you can drive on it at your own risk. It's a four-lane divided highway that follows the coast for about two hours. It's breathtaking. The mountains are right at the sea along the drive so the scenery is simply superb. Many times we would come around a corner and be struck by the simple beauty of the land, the mountains, the sea, and the desert. The drive alone was worth it.

But when we got to the resort we enjoyed an extra bonus: besides us, the only other guests there were a group of ten Italians travelling on a guided tour. They had been to see the turtles laying their eggs the night before and were going to take a night off. Their tour guide, Hilal, offered to take us to watch the turtles lay their eggs. We were thrilled. This area is just beginning to be developed and road signs are rare. We were given a map to find the place with the turtles, but were told not to expect any signs on the roads. It was such a relief to have Hilal take us. Again, just another example of the generosity of the Omani people, so willing to share with others.

The turtle excursion turned out to be an inspirational experience. Green turtles come to a particular beach all year to lay their eggs. It is busiest during the warmer months, but turtles are there all year. We drove out to the sea, checked in at a building, parked the car, and then walked out to meet the guides who would take us to the beach. Our guide shared his knowledge of the phenomenon. I was impressed with the respect in his voice for the turtles and he imparted a sense of honour at witnessing the egg-laying ritual. The turtles are born on this beach and return thirty-seven years later to mate and lay their eggs. (They live to be approximately eighty years of age.) The females burrow holes one metre deep with their front flippers, then nestle into the hole. They lay approximately one hundred golf-ball sized eggs. They cover the eggs with their back flippers and dig another hole the same size, as a decoy for predators, and then they return to the sea. The females lay eggs two or three times before they leave for about two years. Out of one thousand eggs laid, only twenty to thirty hatchlings make it to the sea. I felt as if we were invaders in a very private and divine process. We were given strict orders by our guides: no talking, make a semi circle at the back of the turtle, and no flash allowed when taking photos. If you used a flash you would lose your camera. If you went in front of a turtle, she would be spooked and return to the sea.

We were there an hour in total but it seemed very short. One of the guides pulled a turtle's flipper aside so we could see the eggs being laid. My heart almost stopped beating a few times with humility, and in gratitude for being allowed to observe this ancient ritual. I wondered for how many thousands and thousands of years these turtles had been returning to this beach to mate and lay eggs. One day soon there will be an interpretive centre at that spot on the beach, and scientists from around the world will share their studies and findings with the world.

While Joey was visiting, an exhibition game was to take place featuring the Oman National Football team. An announcement about the game was published in the paper, but with no details on where it was being played or how to get tickets. My son searched the Net and found the home page for the team, but he found no details posted there about the game. We also received no responses to our phone calls. He did discover, however, that their home field was the stadium very close to our house.

The evening of the game, we drove over to the field around seven and the place was absolutely lifeless. We thought that was strange if there was to be a game that night, but with optimism we decided that maybe the game would start later. We went home, waited another hour, and drove back again. Still no activity. In frustration we gave up and decided to go for dinner.

As we cruised down the main road through the city, we saw stadium lights off to our left glaring out at us. Ah! Must be a game of some sort. I quickly veered off the highway and we found our way to the stadium. We parked the car and proceeded to the entrance. Another fan was also heading towards the stadium, so we decided to ask him where to buy tickets. He looked at us strangely and said, "You don't need a ticket!"

Well, that explained why we couldn't find information about tickets, didn't it? Who would have thought the game was free? We entered the stadium and enjoyed the last half of the game. Because it was an exhibition game, there was no scoreboard, so we didn't even know who won the game in the end! But we enjoyed watching it, nevertheless.

On the last day of my friend Dawna's visit to Oman, we returned to the Al Sawadi Resort, the perfect way to spend a last day together. We alternated between relaxing by the pool and swimming in the sea. Life in Oman is so simple and enjoyable, with lots of beaches and resorts to enjoy, and many fine restaurants with delicious, fresh food. Dawna wondered how she would withdraw from the readily available variety of fresh juices. My son, who spent five weeks with me, was as taken with Oman as I am. When he left, he was planning to save some money and come back to secure work and live in Oman for a period of time. He has an easy and quick sense of humour that is a delight. I was thrilled at the prospect of him joining me – it would be so wonderful to have him here. Oman is a very small country and Muscat is a small city of 750,000, a nice-sized city to live in. Whenever you feel you need a big city fix, Dubai is a four-hour drive north or a forty-minute plane ride. If you are a travel bug like I am, there is an endless variety of destinations to explore. Paris, London, Germany are six to eight hours away by air. Thailand, Malaysia, Turkey, Egypt are four hours away. The number of fascinating places to explore on this side of the world is boundless. I was so grateful for the opportunities living in Oman offered.

For Muslims, the beginning of a new calendar month and the end of Ramadan is marked by an event called Eid al-Fitr, which is a time of great celebration and joy for Muslims. And, ironically enough, it coincided with all my company leaving. Ramadan was over, and so was my time as tour guide and hostess. I stayed in my apartment for a whole day following the departure of my guests, sleeping, reading, and watching movies. There was a big shift in consciousness for me at that time. I had been preparing for that shift for quite awhile, wondering what it would be. Monday night I had a very vivid dream with lots of insights into the next stage of my journey – not many details, but at least an understanding it would evolve sooner than later.

I woke up the next morning elated and full of energy. I had been dragging my butt for a while, busy processing inner feelings and messages, and it zapped my strength. What was this "shift in consciousness," you ask? Hard to put into words, but I will give it my best: it was a heightened awareness of all life and how precious each individual is; a new respect for the individual and for each person's unique journey. It was very humbling.

Anyway, I was relieved when Ramadan came to an end. It was an interesting month, with lots of learning on my part. When Ramadan began, the city atmosphere was transformed instantly, with rush hour taking place so much later in the evening, and the city being so quiet during the daylight hours, followed by a hubbub of activity and people at night. The change of pace was refreshing at first. But on the first day after Ramadan ended, I was pleased to be able to go out to a café for breakfast and have a cup of tea. And oh, how I had missed my afternoon tea breaks at work!

My Omani friends.

The Bollywood Dance

By October, my life in Oman had certainly turned a corner. I'd joined two clubs: the American Women's Group and the Women's Guild of Oman. Upon my arrival in Muscat I was advised to join as many groups as possible as a way to get to meet people. Eventually, you would find some you got along with, and friendships would develop. How true that proved to be.

I loved it! Art exhibitions, dancing, parties – oh, I was so happy to be able to say that I actually had a social calendar. One of my first moves was to volunteer for the committee organizing the Halloween party. (Halloween is not celebrated in Oman; many locals do not even know what Halloween is, so the party was strictly an expat celebration.) I spent a couple of hours selling tickets one Thursday morning, and I collected tickets at the door of the event. By then, I knew quite a few people and felt it would be okay to attend the party on my own.

One night, I went to a newcomers' informational meeting at an art exhibition at the Centre for Performing Arts. The Centre also offers a wide variety of dance lessons. Several people at the meeting, including myself, signed up for "cinematic dancing." (I had been taking training in American-style ballroom dancing for fifteen years.) The good news was, you didn't need a dance partner. I looked forward to having dance back in my life.

Cinematic dancing: what is it? As it turns out, cinematic dancing is Bollywood dancing. I had heard the term *Bollywood* before, but I wasn't sure how the term related to dance. I jumped at the opportunity anyway, because I was missing dancing a lot.

So I became a Bollywood dancer, of sorts. After attending eight lessons, I could say with confidence that I was beginning to get it. It kind of reminded me of the jazz dancing lessons I took many years ago. I'm not sure if my years of training in ballroom dancing were a help or a hindrance. Besides all the ballroom rules being broken, there are numerous subtle differences as well, especially in arm movements and how you shift your weight. It's very common in Bollywood dancing not to shift weight from one foot to other during a series of moves of the arms and upper body. After years of ballroom dancing, I automatically shifted my weight with each change in movement. That was difficult to overcome. Sometimes I came home frustrated after a lesson, and sometimes I came home elated. But I soon realized that the same was true with ballroom dancing: frustration, elation. Overall, I was ecstatic with moving my body to music once again. Dancing is like freedom to me. I often compare dancing to feeling like a bird flying through the air. Of course, this is only when I am able to execute the patterns; otherwise it is more like an elephant lumbering through the jungle!

There were about twelve people in the class, including myself. My boyfriend Bob participated, too, while he was visiting. There was one other male in the class. The dancing is not done in partners but as individuals. Bob and I were the only Canadians. The rest of the participants were East Indians, including the instructor. I tried to recruit some of my friends to join, but no luck there. It was natural for the instructor and other participants to speak in Hindi, so I missed a lot. Often, the students would begin a series of patterns, and I didn't even know we were starting because I had missed the cue – minor, but irritating at times. I loved the dancing so much I didn't let that hinder me. I thought I might even pick up a few words and phrases in Hindi.

Our instructor was quite revered by the young students in other dance classes. Those young girls often came in to watch us. They brought the instructor tea and giggled amongst themselves. They were very cute.

One evening while our lesson was underway, the teen-aged girls were preparing for a show. It was captivating to see the costumes, the jewellery, and the elaborate make-up transform those gangly, giggling girls into elegant young women. The experience was very powerful.

The dance lessons also helped me to retrain my brain. Learning the patterns and a different style of dancing is challenging and invigorating. Hurray for Bollywood!

Joining the American Women's Group was a big stretch for me. I'd served as president of Women Business Owners, vice-president of Business Coaches of Manitoba, and president of the Canadian Association of Professional Speakers. How would the American Women's Group compare? The AWG was started by American women who are stationed in the Middle East with their husbands and who wish to get together with other wives for coffee and support. It has become an international organization and serves a great need. Membership in the Oman group is 300. The reason I say it was a stretch for me is because I am a single woman who moved to Oman to work. Initially at meetings, I heard comments such as: "Well, surely everyone has children!" And when some administrative work needed to be done: "Surely one of our husbands can do this for us at his office." Comments like that left me rolling my eyes. Was I really hearing this? Was I really here? Oh, how life does change!

I admire and respect my Omani clients. They are wonderful people and very generous. But I hadn't realized how much I missed the friendship of women from a background similar to mine. By joining the clubs, I believe I have achieved a nice balance. I want to learn about and explore the Oman culture as much as possible. But I also want to maintain contact with my roots.

So by October I began to feel like an old-timer. I had already spent six months discovering Oman on my own. It would have been a lot easier if I'd had access to these women's groups earlier, taking advantage of all the knowledge they had already attained and were so willing to share. Arriving in April proved to be a disadvantage because the groups shut down for the summer. September was busy with membership drives and newcomer events. Activities started in full swing in October. I met many women who'd just arrived and I was grateful to be over the initial difficulties of moving to a new country. Being an old-timer sure felt good!

In October the Omanis observed the first Eid holiday, the Eid El-Fitr, which marks the end of Ramadan. I was invited to spend a day with Ali and his family. I was so pleased to continue to be invited to Ali and Yasmine's home. It was a great honor for me. When I first moved to Oman they were so kind as to include me on a trip to Jebel Shams (Sun Mountain), Al Hoota cave, and Nizwa. After that, I was invited to their home several times. I thoroughly enjoyed those visits. It was so nice to be around a family. Their three daughters were delightful and I became very fond of them.

My dilemma at the beginning was that he has two wives, but I am happy to say Ali allowed me to become comfortable with it. He has a wife in Muscat and one in Sohar. He drives 250 km every day to be fair to both of them. That is very important in Omani culture. He spends alternate weekends with each family and takes both on equal vacations. Ali purchased a piece of land, which he called "the farm," and built two chalet-style villas there, with a swimming pool in between – one villa for each family. Although he calls it a farm, it's quite different from what a prairie person would imagine – two chalets with a swimming pool would hardly be called a farm in western Canada!

I was nervous about going to Ali's on that Eid holiday, because I knew both families would be there. It turned out to be a wonderful day. Ali had just completed the buildings and this was the first weekend the families would be spending on the farm. In addition, it was Eid, a time for family gatherings and celebration. I arrived in the early afternoon and was welcomed to Yasmine's chalet. During the course of the day, many of Ali's family came for a visit. I was honoured to meet his sisters and his mother. His brothers also visited, but remained outside, while I was inside with the ladies, as is the custom. The food was fabulous and I over-indulged a tad.

After a while, Ali took me across the way to meet his second wife. She, of course, was a lovely woman and immediately made me feel at home. They had a young son about two years old, whom I had already met. The children from both wives moved freely between the two houses. However, I still felt a bit uncomfortable with the concept. It was interesting for me to observe myself and my reactions. I noted that both homes were identical, except for the décor; each wife put her personal touch on her home. After refreshments and a short visit, I excused myself and departed for home.

Around that same time, unfortunately, Jackey's family had to face a difficult decision. The boys were registered at an international school that was close to their home, but had a reputation as a very tough school. Both the boys were honour students, but school in Oman was not a happy experience for them. It was very different from their Canadian school environment, with exams every day and an unfamiliar curriculum. It was decided that Fred and the boys would return to Canada in November. It was a sad day for me, but devastating for Jackey. I could feel her disappointment and hurt. It took a few months for both her and me to adjust to life without her family. It took until January for Jackey to start enjoying life once again, but she still found it hard to be without her children. Life is like that.

What are some of the frustrations of living in Muscat?

Well, I have to pay for any repairs made in my rented apartment. Just the way things are here. If something breaks in your apartment and you want it fixed, be prepared to pay for it yourself. If not, it will not get fixed.

For example, my bathroom sink faucet leaked for about six months. I asked repeatedly to have that looked after. "Yes, Madam," was always the response. I said I would pay for the repair, but the reply remained: "Yes, Madam." Then my kitchen tap started to leak. Again, I called the building manager. He came up to look. Success that time, because both the bathroom and kitchen taps were quickly repaired. I still had to pay, though; the bathroom taps had to be replaced, and the kitchen tap needed a washer. Unfortunately, the kitchen tap began leaking again not too long after. After paying the man to fix it, I realized I would have to purchase new kitchen taps, with my own money, and pay him to come again! Frustrating. That's common here. The landlord will not take care of maintenance. Tenants are free, of course, to leave things as they are – broken, leaking, non-functioning. I lived on the third floor and there was no elevator (or *lift*, as they say in Oman). The light in the stairwell never worked when I lived there and I expect it's still not fixed. After all, who would pay for it? What about safety, you might ask – a dark stairwell?

And speaking of apartments – rent is paid six to twelve months in advance. Yes, six to twelve months. I managed to negotiate my payment schedule in four-month increments. Initially, I thought that meant paying a four-month advance, and paying monthly thereafter. Was I surprised when I was told it meant rent had to always be paid in four-month increments! The rental agency told me that landlords had become greedy ever since large companies started paying their employees' rents a year in advance. Landlords now push this and extend it to everyone. I considered myself lucky that I only had to come up with four months' rent at a time. I wondered what young people do who are just beginning their careers. The agent said they have to go to the bank for a loan to pay their rent. And on top of that, tenants have to pay for repairs! But only if they want the repairs made.

Safety standards are very different in Oman. For example, only the people in the front seat of a car have to wear their seatbelts, so it is very common to see the adults belted in the front seat and the children bobbing up and down, playing in the back seat. Yikes!

I cannot even begin to tell about the lack of safety at construction sites: buildings, roadways, and boulevards... It's true, I did see hardhats on *some* roadway construction crews, but it was not the norm. One night when I was driving home, a man was welding on the main street outside a storefront. No goggles, no helmet, nothing – just the sparks flying in the night!

Street cleaners are men who hop out into traffic when there is a break in the traffic and sweep the street with a broom and a dustpan. No motorized street-sweepers here. What is their safety equipment, you ask? Well, congratulations! – they do wear bright orange coveralls, but no hard hats. At least you can spot them quickly, just in case they don't jump back on the curb fast enough!

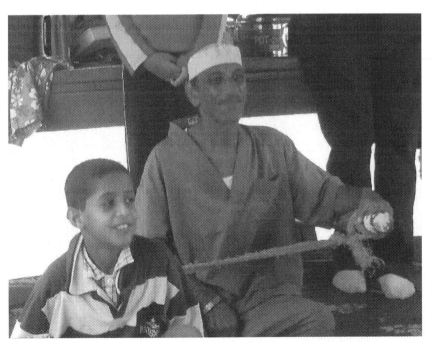

Musandam cruise – captain of the dhow and his grandson.

Late fall, and storm at sea

One day in mid-November of my first year in Oman, I suddenly realized Christmas was just around the corner. I found it difficult to think of Christmas while lying on the beach soaking up the sun. What really reminded me of it at that point was the décor for the upcoming National Day, celebrated in Oman on November eighteenth. The main highway, Sultan Qaboos Street, which runs for sixty km through the middle of the long, narrow city of Muscat, was suddenly festooned with lights and flags from one end to the other. The overpasses were also decorated from top to bottom with lights, with a picture of the Sultan in the middle. Wow! Quite the display. The expression, "all lit up like a Christmas tree," came to mind.

Although November 18th is the official National Day, the actual date of the festivities varies. This is quite common here. Many of the religious holidays depend upon the moon for timing, so they are often announced to the public only the day before. The first year I was in Oman, the National Day holiday took place a week or two after November 18th. I'm not sure why, but that's just the way it was.

And what was making headlines in the newspaper in Oman as December approached? RAIN! Not actual rain, just a slight chance of rain. I had been there for seven months and had seen no form of precipitation whatsoever. So I was very excited to see this headline in the newspaper one day in November:

Rain possible: Muscat

It usually rains once a year, but sometimes not. The forecast did not come true, but just the possibility was exciting. It did, however, rain in Dhofar, which is about 1,000 km from Muscat, at the southern tip of Oman. They generally tend to get more rainfall than Muscat, but the event was still newsworthy.

Faisal, the young man who sometimes served as my Omani representative when required, assisted me in getting my Omani driver's license that November. He was the gentleman who also helped my colleagues and me acquire our residence cards/visas. (Whenever we non-natives had official business with a government office, we had to have an Omani with us.) Obtaining the driver's license was relatively simple process: I gave them my Canadian license, and they gave me back my Omani license. Thank goodness! It's another bonus of being Canadian. Many countries are not so fortunate – their driver's license is not accepted, they have to go through a very long process of testing, taking several months to complete.

Faisal was born and raised in Muscat, which is rare, because most of the Omanis in Muscat today were born in rural Oman and moved to Muscat to work. I don't know Faisal's age, but I guessed he was in his late twenties at the time, or early thirties. He was the eldest of ten children and, as is custom in Oman, he lived at home. His youngest sibling was two years of age. (Faisal's eyes lit up with joy when he mentioned that to me.) At that time, Faisal was the only person in the household providing an income. His father was retired from the Armed Forces. He had a sister and a brother in university in Muscat. Faisal himself did not attend university, but took technical training as an auditor. His true goal, though, was to be his own boss, so he started a small business – graphic design and logo wear. He provides companies with signs and gifts – such as shirts, hats, jackets, brief cases – emblazoned with corporate logos.

That went against his father's wishes. His father wanted Faisal to work as an auditor for the government. But Faisal feels very strongly about being his own boss, and it's a courageous thing for a young Muslim man to do, to go against his father. After two years, Faisal was already experiencing success in his business. He made very good progress.

I asked him if he would be married soon and he broke out in a huge smile. He said that when his sister and brother were finished school and earning an income to contribute to the house, then he would be ready to be married. I asked if he would pick his wife himself, or if his parents would. Another big smile. He said he would pick his wife, but he added that as soon as he was ready, his mother and sisters would begin bringing ladies for him to consider. He said they would be very busy finding him a wife. (Another big smile.)

Faisal is going to need a considerable amount of money to get married. He needs to pay for the wedding, buy a villa, and furnish it. I asked if he thought his wife would work. That caused him some discomfort. He said he would prefer his wife being at home, but realized it was not a popular concept in today's world.

I found Faisal to be a fine young man. I was sure he would have no problem finding a wife. I was also sure he would do very well in the business world.

Those kinds of family traditions are not uncommon in Oman. The eldest boy is responsible for the family. I had two clients here who were the eldest in their families, and they shared the same custom of educating their younger siblings before pursuing marriage and starting families of their own.

I am not suggesting that is unique to Oman, but I am not aware of it being a common practice in Canada anymore.

One day I attended a Holiday Bazaar put on by the American Women's Guild in Oman. It was kind of weird attending a Holiday Bazaar at a five-star resort surrounded by sand instead of snow. Singers entertained the crowd with Christmas carols, and a few tables displayed Christmas decorations. But most of the goods were clothing, jewellery, and artwork. I bought some wonderful cards, depicting the scenery of Oman and the Omani people, to send home as Christmas cards. By the time the bazaar was held, it was much too late to send them to North America in time for Christmas, but I thought the recipients would be delighted, even if the cards were late.

Bob came for a visit in late fall, and I really enjoyed his companionship; he stayed for two months. He had originally said, much to my horror, that he would be going home on December twenty-third. The thought of spending Christmas by myself in Oman was not appealing. How kind of him to change his plans! He got a plane ticket home for January first instead. Much better!

A Canadian gentleman I know here was planning on bringing his family to Oman for Christmas, and we thought we would all celebrate Christmas together, along with Jackey, my co-worker. Alas, his daughter got a job in Egypt where his other daughter was living at the time, so he and his wife chose to go to Egypt for the holidays. One of the daughters is a pastry chef. I had been drooling at the images of the great desserts we would have. But it was not to be. Bob and Jackey and I began making alternative plans, hoping that one of the tourist hotels might put on a Christmas spread for non-Arabic guests. There would be only the three of us, it appeared, since Jackey's family would be returning to Canada before the holiday season began.

One weekend before Christmas, Bob and I took the catamaran *Shinas* to Musandam, a small peninsula owned by Oman. You have to leave the greater part of Oman to get to it. By road it's a ten-hour drive, and you cross the United Arab Emirates border to get to there.

From my research on the Internet:

Shinas, The Sultanate of Oman's 213-ft. vehicle-passenger catamaran, is the world's fastest diesel-powered vehicle passenger ferry after achieving a record service speed of 52 knots and a maximum speed of 55.9 knots (103.5 km/h) during sea trials last November.

The high-speed catamaran Shinas will provide a new tourism service to Oman's spectacular Musandam Peninsula and will be the flagship in the Sultanate of Oman's expanded marine transport network.

As well as having a service speed of over 50 knots, the ferries carry 208 passengers and 56 cars along an intended 180 nautical mile route.

We left mid-afternoon on a Wednesday, the beginning of the weekend here in Oman, and returned Friday night. It was an amazing trip! The fjords and the mountains in Musandam are breathtaking. It's an outdoor person's haven. Not much else is there except exhilarating scenery, so for the shopping tourist – not a good place to visit.

Our adventure began in the waiting room of the terminal. We were told to arrive an hour ahead of time. We did so, and then sat around for forty-five minutes. It was such a typical Oman scene: people talking loudly everywhere; lots of luggage, bags, and boxes scattered throughout the waiting room; men with their entourages – meaning wives and children – in tow. Totally chaotic! Two officials tried to check everyone's tickets, passports, and residence cards, then match up their luggage with their tickets. I just sat back and watched, chuckling to myself at the chaos. Watching line-ups is very amusing here – different culture, different uses of space. The East Indians tend to crowd together, not leaving even a crack of space between themselves and the next person; they don't stand in a line, but create a pack of sorts at the front of the room, or in this case, near the two men trying to check everyone in. The Canadians, Americans, and Brits stand in orderly lines waiting their turn and making sure no one butts into the line. The Omanis just stand very quietly beside the person in charge, not in the line and not in the pack. They wait patiently knowing they will be served as quickly as possible and they always are. It is quite the entertainment.

Finally, after about two-thirds of the crowd was gone, we made our way up to the officials. They checked us in and we were whisked onto a bus to be transported to the port. The port authority required seeing all our passports *again*! Everyone passed them up to the front and the bus driver took them away. To return them to their owners, he simply passed the pile of passports to someone and said, "Pass them back." This made my Canadian hair stand on end! Passports are almost sacred to me. But I managed to find both of our passports and we settled back for the short ride to the ferry.

The *Shinas* is a brand new luxury boat, very roomy and comfortable, with great service. It was a pleasant six-hour ride to our destination. An Omani woman befriended me. She was an English teacher and wanted to practice her English, but had three small children to tend to. The family did not have their maid with them, so although they were busy, she managed to take some time to chat with us.

We arrived at our hotel in the evening and grabbed a quick bite to eat in the hotel restaurant. We booked an all-day dhow cruise for the next day. A *dhow* is a traditional Arabian sailing vessel, though In this case it was powered by an engine, not sails. We depart early in the morning for the cruise. The sun was shining and we were expecting a luxurious day of snorkelling, swimming, and dolphin watching. The scenery was gorgeous. We did encounter dolphins, and our captain, a wizened old Omani gentleman, called them to the boat by whistling. They liked his tune and came to play with us for a while, swimming beside the boat, jumping in and out of the water. Our captain didn't speak much English, but had a ready smile and a joy of living that was delightful. He told us the names of all the small villages we passed. Those villages are accessible only by water. The Oman government supplies fresh drinking water to them weekly. The children attend school and board in Khasab during the week, returning to their villages on the weekends. Fishing is the only source of income for the villagers. Our captain had two young boys helping him, one about eight and one about fourteen. The fourteen-year-old was already an able sailor, adept at manoeuvring his way around the moving dhow – a great help to the captain. The eight-year-old played a fair bit, but every once in awhile was given the rudder. This brought a huge grin to his face. I called him the new captain and I thought he would burst with pride.

Dimaniyat Island.

'Round the bend'

The British, in their inimitable fashion, arrived on this lump of rock called Telegraph Island in the fiords back in the mid-19th century, staying 5 years. They were laying a telegraph cable from India to Basra in Iraq. Taking the cable "round the bend" of the Gulf gave rise to the expression, since living on Telegraph Island in the summer must have sent them crazy.

Source: www.reocities.com

We stopped to snorkel around Telegraph Island. The water was only about 24oC, so it was a little cool, but certainly pleasant. What a great feeling it was to jump off the side of that huge boat into the crystal clear waters.

Suddenly we were being called back to the boat; a strong, cold wind had risen. I was hoping to lie in the warm sun and dry off. Instead, we were thrown into a storm.

We set off from Telegraph Island and found a bit of a sheltered bay in which to sit out the storm. Bob and I were reminded of our many kayaking trips in Canada, getting caught in the rain and finding a sheltered bay or island to wait it out.

Taking into consideration it only rains one to six times per year in Oman, the storm was quite the adventure, complete with thunder and lightning. I had been in Oman seven months and it was my first rainfall. How incredibly exciting! You could see the excitement in the old captain and the young boys as well, their faces lit up with dancing eyes and big smiles. The twelve tourists on the cruise had, however, quite a different perspective. Their day of playing with the dolphins and snorkelling in the clear blue water had come to an abrupt end.

Things went downhill from there. The water got very rough with the strong winds, and the cold rain was dashing all hopes of a leisurely day. The canvas tarp covering the top of the front of the boat tore, allowing the rain to pelt down upon us. We all scurried to the back of the boat, collected whatever cushions we could find and piled them up to shelter us from the cold rain and winds. We all huddled together, looking miserable. But the human spirit prevailed and eventually laughter emerged. The wind died down a bit and I sorted out my space. I pulled Bob's straw hat from underneath me. What was once a proud Western hat was now a flattened mass of straw. It was particularly comical.

Later, one of the gentlemen who had been sitting very comfortably was thrown onto the floor of the dhow when the rough seas bounced him off his cushions. Laughter erupted once we knew he was not hurt. We emerged from the fiord and out into the open sea. Now we knew the meaning of rough seas! It was like a roller coaster, up and down over the huge rolling waves, lots of *oohs* and *aahs*, lots of giggles, as we mounted and descended the huge rollers. There was another dhow in front of us, so we could watch it and see what was coming. Wow!

We arrived back in Khasab very cold and wet, but feeling glad for the adventure. Bob and I were looking forward to a nice hot shower. When we returned to our hotel room we realized we had turned off the water heater. Nothing but cold water! (In Oman, each bathroom has its own water heater. You only need to heat your water in the winter months. Water is stored on top of the buildings and is usually very hot. Most people complain they cannot get any cold water.) So we wrapped ourselves in the spare fleece blankets provided in our room and quickly warmed up. We both fell asleep, and by the time we woke up, there was plenty of hot water for a shower.

The next morning we were off for a mountain safari. Hidal, our Omani guide, picked us up at 9:00. The sun was shining and stayed with us for the day. We ascended narrow winding roads to 1,000 feet above sea level. The mountains were beautiful and the air was incredibly fresh and invigorating. Dotted throughout the mountains were Bedouin villages. As Hidal said, "No wife, no baby, just man." Those places used to be homes, but now the man comes up into the mountains to tend to the goats and returns down the mountain to his family. Hidal stopped at one spot to show us small doors way up in the side of the mountain. The rock was in very large layers and the doors led to caves, former homes of the Bedouins. I wondered how they even managed to climb up to those caves.

We travelled alongside a wadi with terraced gardens. *Wadi* is the Arabic term traditionally referring to a valley, but in some cases it may refer to a dry riverbed that contains water only during times of heavy rain. This wadi still had water in it from the rainstorm the previous day. Hidal told us that for two or three months the wadi is all green and lush on that side of the mountain. The terraced gardens were all fenced. At first I wondered why, and then I remembered the goats, and it made sense: the Bedouin were protecting their gardens from the goats. We stopped atop a mountain overlooking the fiords for a snack of bananas and apples. We delighted in feeding the skins and cores to the goats.

On the trip back to Muscat, the *Shinas* had to stop at sea. She had picked up some plastic bags adrift in the water and needed to clean her engines. Hard to imagine that plastic bags at sea could stop the world's fastest catamaran. It only took fifteen minutes or so and we were up to full speed again.

The trip on *Shinas* cost forty-four Omani rials return each (about $120 at that time). Originally the cost was seventy-two Omani rials, but sales were not as brisk as had been expected, so a discount was in place. A very reasonable price for a luxury journey.

The spoiler at the end of the trip was the announcement that all Omani Nationals would disembark the ship first, followed by foreigners. This seemed so strange to me, but is quite common practice here. Unfortunately, over half of the passengers were foreigners. I did not feel that it was a great way to promote tourism.

The Grand Mosque.

The crystal ball and Eid

In December, I attended my first formal ball in Oman. I understand that winter is indeed the season for such things here. By then, Oman had changed a great deal from when I first arrived in spring. By the time I had moved and was settled in my new apartment, it was mid-May, and events and normal routines had ceased for the summer. There was certainly a flurry of activity now!

The formal ball was a fund-raiser put on by the Women's Guild of Oman. It was an incredible affair. Tickets were fifty Omani rials per person, or about $150. I was accompanied by Bob, Jackey, and a business associate of ours named Tim.

It was billed as a formal event, and it certainly was that. We arrived in the parking lot of the Shangri-La, a five-star resort in a stunning setting. We were greeted by a parking attendant who provided directions. We were instructed to follow the red carpet; it stretched before us, lined with burning candles, flowers, and the smiling, welcoming faces of the hotel staff. This pathway, all lit up by candles, led us directly to the Crystal Ball.

At a reception area we were treated to wine and hors d'oeuvres and serenaded by a symphony of classical music. Shortly thereafter an announcement was made to follow the piper to the banquet hall, and we followed another long stretch of red carpet, candles, flowers, and smiling faces. We entered an open-air amphitheatre, which was elegantly set for a dinner for 700 guests. The palm trees lining the top of the theatre were all decked out in blankets of white lights, which encased the area beautifully. Tables and chairs were tastefully decorated, and flowers and candles adorned the tables. On the way in we were each given a gift from Amouage, a local perfume company. Both men and women were given a box containing five samples of perfume. Amouage perfumes are famous throughout the world. The company will even customize a scent for you. What a delightful gift! (I learned a lot about perfumes while in Oman: how to buy them, how to wear them – a good perfume needs time, so try it on and notice how it changes over time. Perfume reacts differently on everybody, so do some sampling before investing in a good perfume. And by the way, Amouage is a considerable investment.)

There were six other people at our table; four arrived shortly after we did, and two arrived after dinner. One couple was from Germany; when they first introduced themselves, the wife said, "We're from Germany, sorry for the war." He works for Shell Oil and expected his next posting to be Calgary, so we had quite a bit to share with them. The other couple was from Wales; the wife was actually from the interior of China, but had been living in Wales for a long time before arriving in Muscat. He was dressed in a formal kilt. The business associate who accompanied us is from Calgary and still lives there those six months of the year that he's not in Oman.

The conversations were lively and informative. The German couple shared quite a lot of information about trekking in Muscat and the surrounding area. Bob and I love trekking, so were quite pleased. It was so pleasant to be sitting outdoors, looking up at the stars in December and enjoying the balmy evening. The temperature was around 24oC. Most of the men were in tuxedos, the women in long gowns. The dresses were as stunning as the location. I had a long gown made for the occasion, and Bob a new suit. The tailors here are very, *very* good and very, *very* reasonable. The event was mainly attended by expats, but there were a few Omanis in attendance. The expat community comes from all over the world, so many of the gowns were made in different countries – breathtaking beadwork, silks, and laces. A lady told us that Oman is one of the few places in the world where a man can still get good use out of a tuxedo. Apparently, lots of formal balls take place during the winter season, so I could look forward to many more.

After dinner there was an auction of eight items. Two unusual items were two-week vacations in villas in France and Florida. The villa in France created excitement, but not the villa in Florida. As with all charity auctions, the prices went high.

A raffle was held for various items. Two of the prizes were airfare for two, one to the UK and one to anywhere in Europe. We didn't win any of the prizes.

Then we were entertained by a band that had been flown in from the UK. They were a great show band, playing classics from different eras of rock. The lead singer was a woman with an incredibly powerful voice She could really belt out the tunes!

They played for two hours and kept everyone singing and dancing to the oldies. What a wonderful show! Some time after midnight, a DJ took over.

Bob and I arrived home at 2:30 in the morning. We were pretty tired the next day – hadn't stayed up that late in quite a while. During the workweek, my normal wake-up time is 5:30.

Bob and I are ballroom dancers so we were disappointed in the band; they were a show band, not a dance band. The dance floor had a rubber surface, which made any kind of foot movement quite difficult. But we still really liked the show.

All four of us enjoyed the evening immensely – great food, great entertainment, great company, a picture-postcard setting, and balmy weather. Life in Oman is very, *very* easy!

The glamour of the Crystal Ball was followed by the tradition of Eid al-Adha, or, The Feast of Sacrifice, a religious observance in the Arab world that takes place roughly seventy days after the end of Ramadan.

Background:

The boy looks up lovingly at his father, despite the knife in his father's hand – a knife which, he believes, will soon end his life. A grimace of pain is hidden behind the father's beard. The father ignores the ethereal whispers that surround him, coming from the very devil himself, urging him to desist. He knows what must be done. The father looks at the boy, then, slowly, reluctantly, raises his knife to strike the boy down. The strike is never made. Instead, God, who, in order to test Ibrahim's faith, had ordered Ibrahim to kill his son, intervenes, sending an animal to be sacrificed in his place. From this day forth, no human sacrifice would ever be made by the people of the book. And to this day Muslims remember the story of Abrahm on Eid Al Adha.

Source: www.qatarvisitor.com

As with Eid El-Fitr, the holiday is also a time for visiting and greeting friends and family, for eating and for giving presents. An important part of the tradition of Eid is the sacrifice of an animal. I asked many questions about that tradition; what I discovered follows (my version, and I hope I do not offend anyone):

The men of the family will gather at the father's house, each son bringing an animal (in Oman, usually a goat) to be slaughtered. The slaughter is done in the home. Many homes have a specific area dedicated for this ritual. It's important that each man do the killing himself for his family, not one man doing the killing for the greater family. I was not horrified by the details of slaughtering an animal, due to my rural background; my father was a hunter and often butchered meat in our garage. So the killing of an animal was not new to me, but the sacrifice to God was different. I was curious about how many men actually perform this ritual in the Arab world and I got many answers; I gathered that some men do and some don't. It appeared to me that it's more common in the rural areas for the men to slaughter the animal themselves, but as more and more Omanis move to the cities, the tradition is falling away. Many men purchase the animal and have it slaughtered, then share the food as described above.

Building up to the actual day of Eid al-Adha, many goats, sheep, and cows are transported around Muscat in small trucks. It was an unusual sight and caught me off guard at first. Jackey, the animal-lover, was quite distressed. On the day of Eid, we both kept our windows closed. We did not want to hear the sounds of animals dying.

Interesting how cultures and traditions differ, and how individuals react to certain customs. Jackey and I did a presentation for some of our clients. The presentation was followed by lunch with the group. Jackey was sharing her aggravation with dogs barking and fighting at night in her neighbourhood. She lived in the suburbs where stray "wadi dogs" are rampant. The animals are not dangerous, but run in packs that can get quite large, instilling fear in some people. Jackey quite innocently said she had heard you could call the ROP (Royal Oman Police) and they would pick up the dogs.

One of the gentleman, not knowing Jackey's sensitivity to animals, said "Oh yes, they'll pick them up all right!" Everyone laughed at his joke.

Jackey said, "They do pick them up, don't they?"

Another gentleman said, "They shoot them, that shuts them up!"

You could see the horror on Jackey's face. The gentlemen had such fun teasing Jackey after that. The head of the company said he thought the dogs were really witches from Nizwa. Following a long silence, he added, "What dog would bark at a beautiful lady?" Then, with great gusto, he said, "Shoot the buggers!"

And that was the end of the conversation. Jackey did not call the ROP; in fact, a few days later she told me the dogs were only playing when they were barking, not fighting. As if that made it all right.

Bob purchased a *Trekking in Oman* book, and during the Eid holidays we decided to go on a relatively short, two-hour trek inside the limits of Muscat. Assuming it would be an easy hike, we wore sandals.

As we climbed up small trails around a mountain, then traversed down into a riverbed filled with rocks of various sizes, we began to regret our choice of footwear. It was definitely not the easy hike we'd envisioned. At one point, after a steep climb and drinking a fair bit of water to make it up the mountain, it was time for a pee. I chose a secluded spot and proceeded to relieve myself.

Suddenly, we heard a lot of crashing and noise in the underbrush. I thought it was an animal I had scared with my human presence.

But instead, we saw a young Omani man running up the side of the mountain. Oh, I really scared him, all right –

Moslem men are not allowed to see a woman's hair, bare shoulders, or knees. And on top of the egregious sighting of some of my exposed body parts, it happened to be their Holy Day! I wondered what he said at prayers later that day. Bob and I certainly got a good laugh out of the incident, but felt compassion for the young man.

Later on our hike we took a wrong turn and, as we were climbing up a very steep hill, realized we shouldn't be there; it was definitely not a well-beaten path, and both the ascent and descent were a bit uncomfortable. In some way, perhaps the struggle was us being paid back for frightening the living daylights out the young Omani.

Bob and I were both invited for an Eid celebration at Ali's farm. Unfortunately, it was the same day we were leaving for India. I was very disappointed, as I wanted Bob to meet Ali and his family. Luckily, I was able to arrange another, earlier date, and Bob and I travelled to the farm for a barbecue.

We spent an excellent day at "the farm." Ali and Bob played table tennis, and I enjoyed badminton with the three girls. The evening was warm, as usual. Yasmine's house maid, Kokoom, worked for several hours to prepare the skewers for the barbecue, Yasmine used her secret recipe for spicing the meat, Ali's brother, who was also visiting, was responsible for getting the barbecue started, and Ali did the grilling. Notice, Bob and I were responsible for nothing, except to enjoy and eat. And we did a fine job of it, I must say! Ali explained how they purchased the beef from a local farmer and had it butchered locally. I share this to help you understand what kind of man Ali is. He is a very caring and fabulous host. He takes great pride in everything he does and is very generous.

He took both Bob and me on a tour around the property and shared his future plans for additional buildings, guest huts, an airy guest living room with sliding doors and windows that could be closed if needed, aquariums, and a large master bedroom. There are lemon and mango trees on the farm, date palms, and many varieties of vegetables and flowers. It's peaceful and quiet.

Bob and I spent the majority of the time with Yasmine and the girls. During the early evening Ali invited us to say hello to his second wife in her villa. She by then had a new baby girl, and I was thrilled to be able to hold the baby for a while. She was one month old. I was watching Bob to see what his reaction was, but he didn't reveal anything. I asked him later what he thought of the two wives at the farm. He didn't say a lot, but said he was okay with it.

It was interesting to me how much more comfortable I was the second time. It seemed completely natural, quite a switch from my original thoughts. The more time I spent in Oman, the more I realized that people are just people, no matter where you are and what their customs are. Most often, at least in my experience, the people are delightful!

As winter progressed, I began to lose my Canadian hardiness. The temperatures dropped to 20-22 degrees C in the evening – comfortable, right? But I found it a tad chilly – Yes chilly! I actually had to put on a light jacket or sweater to sit outside in the evening. I realized it was December in Canada, too, and in talking to my sister and my son there just before Christmas, discovered that the temperatures had dropped to −44oC in some places. I was so grateful to be in Oman!

The view of the Ganges River from our hotel.

India!

During the Eid holiday, Bob and I went to India for five days to raft down the Ganges River. What an awesome trip, like being transported to another dimension.

I arranged the trip through an agent in Oman and everything went very smoothly, except for a long delay in our departure from the Muscat airport – 4:30 AM instead of the scheduled 2 AM. We were forced to spend a rather restless night in the airport, waiting for our flight to take off. Upon our arrival in New Delhi, a representative from the tour company met us and welcomed us to India. He then escorted us to the pick-up place where we met our driver, Ashok. We spent the next four days with Ashok. He was a real gem.

Our destination was the town of Haridwar, where we would be staying during our rafting excursions. It was only 200 km away, but the drive took six hours. Yes, six hours! Driving in India presents many challenges.

Firstly, twenty-two million people live in the area. That puts a lot of cars on the road. And the road is used by many types of transport, not just motor vehicles. In addition to cars, trucks, motorcycles, scooters and the unique three-wheel taxis, there are cows, oxen, people, horses, and tractors, some carrying varying amounts of goods and people. The questions that kept coming to mind were: how many people can you fit on a bicycle? A scooter? A motorcycle? In a three-wheel taxi? Is that really legal, three people riding on the bumper? One day while we were getting gasoline for the car (gas can be bought only ten litres at a time), I was observing one of the transport trucks idling nearby – six people in the cab, and the driver's seat empty. To my amazement, another man slipped into the cab, but he wasn't the driver, either. For Westerners, the term "personal space" takes on a whole new concept; it simply does not exist. (I began to notice the cultural difference in personal space in other places also. Even at the airport in Oman, people from India do not line up at the customs desk; they pack themselves around it like sardines. There's lots of room and the line-up is short, but they prefer to be packed together really tight.)

And then there are the accidents on the highways. We encountered three accidents in the first ten minutes of our drive. One was between a motorcycle and a car; there was a heated argument going on at that accident scene, people hitting each other with their fists. Yikes. Our eyes bugged out of our heads, I'm sure. After seeing a different motorcycle turn in front of four lanes of on-coming traffic, I let out a "Holy crap!" Ashok started to laugh. He said that in India you need only three things to drive: a good horn, good brakes, and good luck. That motorcycle made it, no collision. The other drivers had good brakes and good horns, and he had good luck. Anything is possible in India.

Horn honking is constant – you just get used to it and don't notice it after a while. I watched Ashok and at times he would honk the horn even when there was nobody near us. Habit, I guess. I now understood the driving in Oman a little better. A very large portion of the expat population there is East Indian. It made me see that driving techniques in Oman were child's play compared to those in India. I wondered what I would think of driving in Canada when I returned. Would I be frustrated with the order instead of the chaos? I was very grateful for our driver and his driving skills. We arrived safe and sound in Haridwar.

My tour brochure said:

Haridwar or 'the Gateway to the Gods' is one of the seven holiest places according to Hindu mythology, as the Gods are believed to have left their footprints in Haridwar. Due to its geographical location too, Haridwar stands as the gateway to the other three important pilgrimages of Uttrakhand, namely, Rishikesh, Badrinath and Kedarnath. Referred to as Mayapuri, Gangadwar, and Mokshadwar in the ancient scriptures and epics, Haridwar has always remained a major pilgrimage for the Hindus.

We could feel a shift in energy as soon as we entered the city, a peaceful atmosphere.

Ashok had to stop and ask directions to our hotel several times. Finally a rickshaw driver led us to an empty gravel lot in the midst of the city. We were met there by a rickshaw driver from our hotel. He took us on a five-minute ride through very narrow alleys lined with shops of all descriptions. Cows, monkeys, people, bicycles, motorcycles and rickshaws all used those narrow passageways.

Our hotel, the Haveli Hari Ganga, was small, charming, simple, and elegant. I had been worried; our travel agent said to be prepared, the hotel isn't five-star. I thought it was far better than a typical five-star.

Upon arrival we were each presented with a necklace representing the god Shiva. We then proceeded to our room for some much-needed rest, since it had been thirty-six hours since we'd last slept. A few hours later we went down for supper. Actually, it was the entertainment in the lobby that woke us up. Two men were performing, one on a hand-drum, and one on an instrument that was like an accordion that sits on the floor. One of the musicians was singing songs native to the area.

Supper was a vegetarian buffet, an incredible taste explosion. Dessert and chai tea (ginger masala) followed. Haridwar is a vegetarian city – no meat, dairy, or eggs.

Then we returned to our room looking forward to a good, solid night's sleep. The lock for the room was a monstrous padlock – quaint and fun. The room was all marble and very cold. Fortunately, the hotel provided an electric space heater. There was a sign in the room: "Water is a precious resource. There are two buckets of hot water in reserve and then it takes thirty minutes to heat up." We had a heavenly hot shower before retiring. The space heater began to warm up both the floor and the marble slab that formed the platform for our mattresses. I was enamoured with the room. The light fixtures were stained glass, and everything was so simple and yet so classy.

Day Two

After early rising early and taking another hot shower, we wondered what breakfast held in store for us. Again, it turned out to be delicious – vegetarian and exquisite. I would love to name the dishes we were served, but I don't know them, except by their obvious components, such as pea sprouts with lime, herbed potatoes, coconut sauce, creamed tomato sauce with a rice ball, stir-fried veggies and other unidentifiable but tasty wok-fried items, and *dhal* (lentil sauce) with rice. At one point a chef arrived in the dining room, and on a very large griddle he fried a crisp and tasty pancake. We also had some kind of porridge that looked like cream of wheat, but tasted much better, sweet and truly creamy. I asked for toast and got it, but how boring that was! Due to the old Canadian politeness, I forced myself to eat it, since I had, after all, ordered it.

(One time I ordered tea in the hotel room. Two men delivered it. I mistakenly gave them Omani money. They were confused but oh, so polite. I changed the Omani funds to Indian rupees and everyone was happy. But the expressions on their faces when they looked at the Omani money was quite comical and I had a good laugh, as did they.)

After breakfast, we asked the rickshaw driver to take us to the parking lot to meet Ashok. The rickshaw driver was small and one of the streets very steep, so Bob and I got off and walked up the hill, then got on again. I think the rickshaw driver was a little embarrassed, but grateful. Ashok was not at the lot when we arrived, but another driver from our Delhi tour company was. He assured us Ashok was on his way.

As Ashok manoeuvred the car to our next destination, I began calling him The Amazing Ashok, for his navigating the roads so well. It was an hour's drive to Rishikesh, where we picked up the representative from the rafting company and began ascending one of the Himalayan mountains.

> *Rishikesh, around 28 km off Haridwar, is at the base of the Himalayas and it is where the Ganges comes down to the plains from the hills. A breathtaking experience of natural beauty and undiscovered wildlife awaits here. Not to mention the peace and tranquillity of a landscape associated with sages and meditation.*

Yikes! – narrow roads up the mountain and lots of trucks and buses coming down. I didn't think there was enough room for passing, but of course, there always was. I found it better not to look at the road, but to watch the Ganga (Ganges, in English) valley unfold along the way.

At the rafting pick-up point, the guide we met there explained that, due to recent violence in Mumbai, the tourism in the area was slower than usual. Normally, the pick-up point would be teeming with people. Lots of Indian companies paid for camping and rafting trips for their staff, but a change in economy meant cut-backs, and paid holiday trips were among the first things to go. So, Bob and I were the only two in our boat, besides the two guides. Two other boats left at the same time as we did, and they each had twelve people per boat. Our guides hooked up an oar system to the middle of the raft and we sat in the front where we had a bird's-eye view.

Our river rafting guide, Karan.

What a great adventure it was! A few of the rapids were what experienced rafters refer to as Class IV – exhilarating and fun, fun, fun. The water was cold, though, and our bird's-eye view quickly turned into a very wet bird's-eye view. The drenching of cold water, which happened often in the rapids, took our breath away. The river route took us through the lower Himalayas and back to the town of Rishikesh. The whole trip lasted about four hours, including a stop for lunch at one of the camps. At one point, we saw from our raft about twenty monkeys frolicking on the shoreline. Apparently, wild elephants, leopards, and deer live in the mountains, but we didn't see any of them.

Our raft/rapids guide was Karan, a young man in his twenties from Nepal. His helper mostly stayed in the background and didn't talk much. Karan's English was quite good. He told us he worked ten months serving as a rafting guide, then two months back home with his mom and sister. He also had one sister in India. He was a very pleasant young man and an expert on the rapids. He had an appreciation for humour as well. Near the end of the river trip, he offered to take a picture of Bob and me. I pretended to push Bob into the water. Karan thought that was really funny.

Because it was a beautiful day, sunny and warm, with temperatures around 20oC, we were able to warm up and dry out by doing a little paddling. The camp where we stopped for lunch, one of forty-six camps this tour company has in the mountains, was very pleasant. We had rice with dhal, vegetables, potatoes, and two kinds of flatbreads. We sat in comfortable rattan chairs, enjoyed our lunch, and watched the Ganga flow by. After we finished eating, Karan joined us for a chat. He explained that the camp he stayed at was a deluxe camp with toilets and showers in the rooms. The camp we stopped at had tents, for short-term stays by tourists.

At the end of the river trip, when we paddled through Rishikesh, we passed lots of temples, ashrams, and yoga schools. Rishikesh is known as the world centre for yoga gurus. The Ganga is considered a holy river by the Hindus. Our river guides, both Hindus, said prayers before we started our journey. Haridwar, where our hotel was, is the holy city where the Hindus float the burning bodies of the deceased in the water, a return to the god Shiva.

Now, one would think the adventure was over for the day, but no. Ashok picked us up and manoeuvred the roads once again. He stopped and asked us if we wanted to buy anything. We said yes, and he turned around and took us to a store that was a government-sponsored co-operative in the area. Lots of statues of Hindu gods were on display, made of bronze, silver, and gold. One of store clerks showed us bolts of silk. At first I didn't understand what those bolts of cloth were. He kept saying, "Blouse, blouse." I knew I was missing something, as the piece of silk was at least four meters long. Finally Ashok rescued me and translated; the piece of cloth was for a sari. I asked how I could get a sari made; much discussion followed, in Hindi, and voila! Ashok said it could be arranged for me to have one by the next day. I chose a purple fabric with a silver border. The cost was 2600 Indian rupees, or about sixty Canadian dollars. Ashok said that in New Delhi, it would cost 7000 rupees to have a sari made.

Another clerk from the store joined us and we were off to the tailor's for measuring. We followed a small alleyway. The tailor's establishment consisted of a front counter and two sewing machines, staffed by a gentleman with white hair, a middle-aged lady, and two teenaged girls. The whole shop was about the size of a closet. My measurements were taken, and I was informed I would also need an undergarment to wear with the sari. More measuring and another 400 Indian rupees. When the tailor said 400 rupees, he expected me to barter, the normal way to shop in India. When I just said yes, his eyes lit up and he grinned from ear to ear. For the remainder of the time we were there, he just kept grinning. I believe I made his day. His big, broad smile was a great gift for me.

Ashok delivered Bob and me back to the hotel parking lot where our rickshaw driver awaited. He took us to the hotel, but his time the narrow alleyways were more crowded than ever, and he had to stop often to avoid hitting people. Once at the hotel we ordered tea, wonderful masala tea. I took a hot shower because we were still chilled from sitting in clothing wet from rafting. Bob wrapped himself up in blankets and was soon in dreamland. The gentleman from the spa in the hotel stopped by our room to see if we wished to use the services. Oh, yeah! I went for a wonderful ayurvedic massage, followed by a steam sauna. Wonderful, wonderful! After Bob got up, he decided to try an ayurvedic wrap, but didn't enjoy it.

Back in the room later, we heard the musicians playing, so we knew it must be time for yet another exquisite meal.

Day Three

The next morning we went higher up the Himalayas and rafted down. We were joined by a young man from Australia. He was taking a year-long, round-the-world journey which began in January, 2008, and would finish in January, 2009. His next stop was to be Japan. His visit to Canada had included Vancouver, Whistler, and Calgary. It was his first and only day of rafting.

Karan was our guide again – what a charming young man. I chatted a fair bit with him this time, since I gave up my exclusive front seat to the Australian. Karan was twenty-two years old. He supported his mother and sister in Nepal. His sister was still at home, only twelve years old; the custom was that she had to finish school before he could marry. When he had saved enough money – around twenty-six years of age, he expected – his mother would find him a wife. As a married man, he would guide for six months only, and spend six months at home in Nepal. He had been working since he was twelve when his father died. We were very blessed to have Karan as our rafting guide for two days.

The young Australian fellow shared an interesting story about Rishikesh. It became famous as the place where the Beatles spent six months in an ashram. They apparently wrote the *White Album* during their stay there. It's rumoured that they left for two reasons: one, Ringo and his girlfriend were tired of India, and two, the Yogi Master at the ashram was getting greedy, asking for more and more money and fooling around with the girls in the Beatles' entourage.

The rafting was very cold that day. We body-surfed one of the rapids, called the Roller Coaster – no huge rocks, so it was fun rolling up and down with the very large waves. Yahoo! But the water was really frigid and we were chilled to the bone after that. I would have loved to go cliff-diving, but it was just too darned cold. Nobody went cliff-diving.

I picked up my sari at the tailor's. It was beautiful! But how do you wear a sari? I decided to search the Net when I returned to Oman. I would also ask my massage therapist, Loveleen; she was from Kashmir, and I am pretty sure she would know how to put it together.

We'd hoped to go to one of the two famous temples in Haridwar that night, but they were closed to the public due to it being Sunday, their holy day. The next day, Ashok would be picking us up first thing in the morning to return to Delhi, a harrowing six-hour drive, so we'd have no chance to go to the temple the next day, either. In the parking lot, we happened to meet Ashok's son, a doctor, who had stopped by to visit his dad. You could see on the son's face the love and respect he had for his father. It was heart-warming.

We returned to New Delhi via the same obstacle course. We stopped for lunch at the same place as on our way up. The waiter not only recognized us, but actually remembered what we had ordered, and asked us if we wanted the same thing. It struck us then that we had seen few other Western people in the last four days; Bob and I were an anomaly.

We met our City Guide and began a tour of Delhi.

Delhi, where an empire rose and fell before the dawn of history; where citadels of emperors appeared and disappeared; a city of mysterious eternity whose old ruins proclaim a majestic and imperial past and whose present pulsates vibrantly with the ever flowing life of India. The eternal Jamuna bears witness to the glorious and tumultuous 5,000 year old history of Delhi. A history which begins with the creation of Indraprastha by the Pandavas and the transformation of this barren gift of the Kauravas into an idyllic haven. A history which encompasses all the various kings and emperors who fixed their royal citadels here – Indraprastha, Lal Kot, Quila Rai Pithora, Siri, Jahanpanah, Tughlakabad, Ferozabad, Dinpanah, Delhi Sher Shahi or then Shahjahanabad. But, combined and integrated into one, these 'new cities' have always been called Delhi and howsoever many names it may have acquired, Delhi has always been intrinsically identified with power and imperial sway. There have been at least eight cities around modern Delhi, and the old saying that whoever founds a new city at Delhi will lose it has come true every time – most recently for the British who founded New Delhi in 1911.

Source: www.delhitourism.com

After driving past the squalor and garbage along the roadways and in the rural areas, New Delhi was very refreshing, clean, and green – at least, in the tourist locations. We could see the British influence in the stately gardens. India was considered the Jewel in the Crown of the British Empire.

Our city tour guide provided us with these nuggets of cultural information:

–Seventy percent of India's population rents, they do not own property.

–The caste system still exists.

–In rural areas, marriages are still arranged, but for city dwellers, that tradition is often not possible.

–People must marry within their caste.

–Delhi was originally seven cities that amalgamated into New Delhi.

–The population is eighteen million, but more like twenty-two million when three satellite cities are included.

We visited the Parliament House; a forty-two-meter-high stone arch of triumph called the India Gate, which is a monument to soldiers of the Indian Army fallen in various wars; sites called *ghats* along the Jamuna River where important leaders such as Mahatma Ghandi were cremated; a red sandstone structure called Hamayun's Tomb, considered to be the forerunner of the Taj Mahal and an epitome of Mughal architecture; the Jama Masjid, one of the largest and oldest mosques in India, where one is allowed to climb up to the minarets for a fantastic view of the city below.

I felt I would like to take another trip to India to discover the rest of the history and beauty of New Delhi. It's considered to be one of the cities of the Golden Triangle, and I think a Golden Triangle trip would be wonderful.

We stayed overnight in New Delhi before flying out early the next morning. We had another superb dinner at the hotel, with meat this time, which I admit I had begun to miss.

But I'll never forget that first six-hour drive from New Delhi to Hradiwar. It was incredible – the sights, the sounds, the smells. I was reluctant to come to India, but curious at the same time. I have met several people who have travelled to India and fallen in love with the country. I could see why. It is exotic and alluring. The myriad of human existence is incredible, from absolute poverty to absolute wealth. Yet there is gentleness there. After searching for quite a while for a word to describe my thoughts on India, humbling was the world that fit the best. I was humbled by her beauty, humbled by her poverty, and humbled by her spirit.

After the cooler Indian climate, I found Muscat uncomfortably warm upon returning. But it took only a day to get used to the heat again – no need for sweaters and warm shawls.

On the road to Haridwar.

Linda, Benita, Jackey, Donna.

The New Year,
and visitors from Saskatoon

On December 28th and 29th all the leaders of Gulf coast countries met in Oman for the thirteenth annual Leaders' Summit.

Wow! – mind-boggling security. The first day, Sultan Qaboos Highway was closed to traffic from 8 AM until 3 PM; and on the second day, from 3 PM until 10 PM. Because Sultan Qaboos Highway is a major road carrying ninety percent of the traffic through the city, I thought the closures would create absolute chaos. But in his wisdom, His Excellency the Sultan closed all the government offices for those two days, and many private firms followed his lead. The roads were relatively clear, as most people stayed home.

We wondered why the road was closed instead of the kings and rulers being brought in by helicopter. Al Bustan Palace Hotel, where the summit was held, has a helicopter pad. A long time resident of Oman shared with me that, in the past, many members of royalty and their families have been killed in attacks on their helicopters. The papers were full of news of the event and it went off without a hitch, or at least without a hitch we know about.

Jackey made a comment about all the military equipment and troops posted around the city. She found it a bit unsettling. It was an interesting awareness for me. In Winnipeg, it is not uncommon to see soldiers heading out of the city in full battle gear. We have a huge air force base in the west end of the city and, until recently, training bases and barracks for the military within the city limits, with additional facilities an hour's drive away. It wasn't unusual for me to see military personnel, and I didn't find it unsettling to see soldiers posted around Muscat.

Bob and I took a trip out of Muscat to visit friends on a farm on Dec. 29th, and on the way back to Muscat there was an army checkpoint set up.

They did not ask any questions or even fully stop us; they just slowed traffic down and gave the vehicles a cursory glance.

I was very happy, however, when the GCC Summit was over and life in the city returned to normal.

Bob and I celebrated New Year's Eve at one of the tourist hotels here, the Radisson SAS in Al Khuwair. It was fabulous – a poolside venue and another splendid evening. The temperature was down to about 22oC – very pleasant. The band was great, the setting lovely, and the food plentiful – not the best food I'd had, but a lot of variety and quantity. Mostly non-Omanis attended the event, as New Year's Eve is not celebrated in Arab countries. (The Arabian New Year's Day fell on December 28th and was celebrated with special prayers and poetry readings at the mosques.) There were a few Omanis present at the Radisson party, but most of the attendees were expats.

In Dubai, all the New Year's Eve events were cancelled a few days before the event, and in Qatar, the hotels, bars, and clubs hosting celebrations were closed down at 11:30 PM. My big question was, why? I had brunch with a friend a few days later and he explained that this was a political move to show solidarity with Palestinians in light of a recent round of hostilities in the Gaza Strip.

The next big happening in Muscat was the bi-annual competition for the nineteenth Gulf Cup: yes, football! (Soccer, if you're Canadian.) In the days leading up to it, many of the streets were festooned with streamers in the country's colours: green, red, and white; homes as well as cars were decorated with flags and streamers and banners depicting stars, flags, the Gulf Cup logo, pictures of the team. Many cars were completely covered in stickers, and some car owners even painted the bodies of their vehicles. The football fans were ready for the big event, which ran January 4th to 17th. It all reminded me a little of the Grey Cup in Canada.

During the actual games and festivities, football fans were dressed in green, red, and white, and many faces and bodies were painted in those colours, with lots of wigs, horns, flags, and so on.

Although I did not attend any games, I did wonder about tickets, after the experience my son Joey and I had had the previous summer when we tried to find tickets for an exhibition game. Tickets to Gulf Cup games were sold only the day of each game, starting three hours beforehand, and all rush seating. I can only imagine what kind of chaos that was. The stadium, I understand, holds a mere 25,000 fans. I heard reports later that the parking lot was full and the streets around the stadium were lined with cars. Had my son been here, we would have taken in some games, but I elected to watch them on TV – no black-outs!

The day of the final arrived, and to my amazement, admission to that game was free. Yes, free, no charge! That really challenged what I call "my Canadianism."

And, it happened: Oman won the 2009 Gulf Cup! It was the first win for them and it took thirty-eight years to happen. The celebration was fabulous. The night the big win took place was really something to witness. Fans were out on the streets until three and four in the morning, cheering from their cars, hanging out the windows and sun roofs, dancing in the streets, greeting everyone and sharing the victory. The energy in the air was exciting and full of joy. The horns did not stop honking until the wee hours of the night. Traffic in most places was at a standstill. The Sultan proclaimed the following day a holiday in honour of the win.

The football team became overnight heroes. Weeks later they were still receiving awards and money, in addition to receiving many gifts from corporations in Oman, including cars and apartments.

The fascinating thing about it was that all that celebrating took place without liquor. Muslims, generally, do not drink, which made the celebrations even more interesting – no problems with all the stupidity that comes with drunken fans, the fights and harsh words – just pure celebration that everyone shared in, all ages and all nationalities. It was reported in the paper how wonderful it was to see many expats dancing in the streets to celebrate the victory – genuine enjoyment and fun for all.

At the same time as all that excitement and festivity unfolded, I was anticipating the arrival of my friends from Saskatoon, who were coming to see me, their old buddy, in Oman.

For those of you unfamiliar with Canada, Saskatoon is a small but charming city nestled in a river valley in the northern part of the province of Saskatchewan. Its population is about 350,000. My friend Linda is a superintendent in the Saskatoon public school system, and my friend Donna runs a networking/marketing business, Usana Health Sciences. We have been through thick and thin together. Even though it had been fourteen years since I'd lived in Saskatoon, we three had remained very close. Linda and Donna have come to visit me wherever I have been living. I was so excited to have them visit me in the Middle East.

It was interesting to see Muscat and Oman through their eyes. I continue to be surprised at how many untruths exist in people's minds about life and inhabitants here. Canadians who have had no direct experience with the Middle East rely mainly on media reports, and a lot of those reports are about terrorists and war, a very small part of what goes on; the "bad guys" get the most coverage. Donna and Linda had many of the same thoughts as I did when I first arrived. Many people told them to very careful and asked if they were sure it was safe to travel to Oman. For women, there is the added concern about what to wear. You are told, "Shoulders and knees need to be covered," but until you arrive, you don't really know what that means. Is it okay to wear open shoes? And is it okay to wear red polish on your toes? Gentlemen, those questions may baffle you, but the women reading this will understand.

I was delighted that both Linda and Donna fell in love with my temporary home, as had I. Linda's statement was, "I am going home and telling everyone about how great Oman is. I am busting the myths!" The beauty of Oman and its people is breathtaking.

We spent most of our time in Muscat, but did get out to rural areas a bit. We also spent three nights in Dubai. I had discovered that if your first trip to the Middle East is Dubai, you think Dubai is very Middle Eastern. But if you have come to Oman first, which is a lot more traditional, you find Dubai quite Western. Both Linda and Donna found that to be true, also.

Another interesting twist is clothing. The Omani men wear the *dishdashas* and the ladies the *abayas*; sounds boring – always the same – but it isn't. The Omani people are always well-dressed – no T-shirts or ripped-up jeans. Everyone is clean and pressed at all times. It's actually quite bewildering how a man can keep his white dishdasha so spotless. On our safari in Dubai, Linda asked our guide about his dishdasha and he proudly told her he owned forty-eight of them. Most of the women have decorative embroidery and/or sequins on their headscarves (*sheylas*), or at the end of the arm of their abayas – not all, but most. After a few days here, Linda commented on how under-accessorized she felt. I felt that, too, when I first arrived. As I tried to adapt, Jackey made jokes about me, saying I'd really discovered the bling. You do tend to kick it up a notch!

Linda is an extrovert and Donna an introvert. Linda was always talking to the Omani people, asking questions about their jobs, lives, and families. I listened in and discovered that most of the questions she asked were the same questions I'd asked when I arrived. That was comforting to me. Our friend Donna managed to survive twelve days with two extroverts. She even managed to sneak in some quiet time for herself in those days. I think she appreciated the low-key culture in Oman.

It was a bit overwhelming at first for Linda and Donna – the different culture and language and a bigger city, but they both adapted quickly and really enjoyed their holiday. I was so happy to have them here. There was a lot of smiling going on for those twelve days!

Every weekend, Thursday and Friday, in the little town of Nizwa, nestled between the desert and the mountains, the goat souq unfolds. Goat meat is a regular on the Omani table, but is not a common item on restaurant menus, and I wasn't keen on trying it.

(When I was invited to Ali's farm for lunch during the Eid holiday in

October, I did eat one of the best meat dishes I'd ever had. It was a traditional Eid dish. The meat is marinated in spices, a fire pit is dug, the fire lit, and the meat is added and covered. The meat is cooked very slowly over a few days. I didn't know if they'd prepared goat or lamb, neither of which I would normally eat. But Ali, Yasmine, and the girls were raving about how delicious the dish was, so I decided to try it. It was fabulous! So tender and succulent. I never did find out what animal it came from.)

I first heard about the goat souq adventure from another expat in Oman – one of those things you just have to know about; there is no publicity about it, and no directional signs to get you there. It begins at about 7:00 in the morning, when the villagers come down from the surrounding mountains to sell their goats. The trucks with the goats on board begin to collect in the parking lot, the creatures are herded into the auction area, and many greetings are exchanged. I have been told that the women, in fact, own the goats. The men do the selling while the women are on the sidelines, collecting the money. The circular parade of goats begins at 8 AM. I'm not sure exactly how this transpires, as the proceedings are in Arabic. Although there doesn't seem to be any order to the procedure, all the animals are sold in a few hours; you see money exchanging hands and goats proudly being taken away by the new owners. I couldn't identify any one person organizing the event, just hundreds of people milling about, yelling, bartering, smiling, and laughing.

I visited the goat souq more than once and found it entertaining each time. I decided to take Linda and Donna to see it. They said, "It's just like the National Geographic!" What a great description. You definitely know you are a visitor there.

The goat souq is a very colourful event: the men in their white and tan dish-dashas and the ladies on the sideline often dressed in the traditional wear of their region, rather than the black abaya. The traditional wear is a tunic and pants of many bright colours and designs. Those ladies often wear face masks made of leather to protect their faces and eyes from the winds and the blowing sands.

The goats are various sizes and colours. Some are baby goats, or kids, and are carried around the circle. They are so cute! Many of the goats aren't very happy about being on display. I wondered if they knew their next destination: the dinner table. Often the men have to drag them around; they straighten their front legs and put their heads down. It was hilarious to me as an onlooker, but I could also see that the men didn't find it funny as they struggled to get the goats moving. It was interesting to watch that very traditional Omani event, but I noticed one rather funny thing: the men parading the goats around and the buyers on the sidelines were using cell phones – a strange configuration of the old and the new.

The ninety-minute drive to the goat souq is itself interesting, since there are many things to see in the surrounding area, making it a worthwhile destination.

During their visit, I would look at my two dear friends and smile in astonishment. Twenty years ago, when we first began our friendship, who would ever have imagined us in Nizwa, for example, half-way around the world, enjoying a traditional goat souq? When our children were young and we were beginning our careers, we banded together in times of troubles. It was wonderful to ponder on how things had changed. Our children were grown, our careers had taken many different directions, and times were very good. Two of us were single and one married when we met; twenty years later, two of us were still single and one married, but it was a different person who was married. Life is so fascinating!

Middle East news and expat culture

While in Oman, I regularly purchase a magazine called *Arabian Business*. It helps me to understand the political, business, economic, and social environments of the Middle East. I read a fascinating article in one issue: "Saudi Arabia tests the water on reform."

According to the article, Saudi Arabia allowed a low-key return of cinema – after a nearly thirty-year hiatus – with the premier of a locally produced comedy movie, screened before mixed-gender audiences. (Strict Islamic rules ban unrelated men and women from mixing.) This bold move was originally rejected by the hard-line morality police, but they later backtracked. The article said the screening of the comedy was "more than a symbolic gesture and could eventually see the conservative Kingdom's ruler contemplate bolder reforms." Khaled al-Dakhil, a political sociology professor at King Saud University, was quoted as saying, "It shows a giant step for the Saudi society as a whole."

I also found out that, according to the *Arabian Business* article, Saudi Arabia is the biggest and most populated Gulf Arab state, but has the lowest gross domestic product per capita. "Most of its seventeen-and-a-half million citizens share little of the ruling elite's fabulous wealth."

I wondered how significant that was until I read the following statement: "In the long run, analysts say, the Kingdom will have to enact deeper reforms than cinema, including fairer wealth distribution, and improved public and political freedoms, to ensure young people do not fall under the sway of religious militants."

Saudi Arabia is, by the way, a place where women are not allowed to drive. I spoke with an expat in Muscat who had just come from a posting in Saudi Arabia with her husband. I asked her what it was like to be an American woman there. She said you have to make the best of things. She draped herself in an abaya as required by law. The good thing about that was, she did not have to worry about what to wear in public anymore! Under her abaya she could have comfortable pyjamas on and nobody would know. I asked about not being able to drive. She said it wasn't all that bad being chauffeured around all the time. I thought about it for a while and wondered how many of the wealthy people in the world actually drive themselves. My guess is, not very many. Of course, this lady I mentioned was fortunate to have a driver. The majority of the Saudi women do not.

I listened on the Internet to an interview with Andrew Cohen, who considers himself a modern day spiritual teacher, and he said something that really hit home for me. He was speaking about the way the world is changing, and one of the things he talked about was the new global economy. We are now seeing how all countries and cultures are linked together economically. To me, the recent financial crisis really illustrated that. He suggested that our next step is to get connected culturally and socially as well. (At least, that is my interpretation of what he said.)

A fascinating thought! What kinds of changes have to happen in the world for us to become one as human beings, instead of as economic units? I found the article on reform in Saudi Arabia fascinating, in light of thinking of all people as one. I also wondered: is the change happening already? It certainly was for me. My experiences in the Middle East have expanded me as a human being. People and customs that had been foreign to me became familiar. I was pleased to be able to place myself in the new global concept of the world and its inhabitants.

In early spring of 2009, I was blessed to have my sister Wendy come visit me. I felt tremendous pride as I introduced her to my new life in Oman. Wendy and I are only two-and-a-half years apart in age and are very close. Our lifestyles are quite different, but our common family bond and love keep us together.

Her stay here was busy, as time was limited and there was a lot to experience. Wendy quickly fell in love with this country, just as I did.

There are two experiences I want to describe:

One evening we went down to the Traditional Souq. I introduced her to the vendors I usually deal with. It's like going for a visit – we catch up on news about families, they offer refreshments. The souq consists of hundreds of small shops, and most of them carry the same goods. I determine where to shop based on how I feel about the owners. Bartering for price is a normal part of business at the souq and Westerners need to get used to this way of shopping. At one of the shops we usually visit, the owner gave each of us a gift, a scarf. My sister was quite taken aback; she said that was the first time in her life she'd received a gift from a store-owner!

A few days later she had another shifting experience. I was busy at work all day, so she decided to walk down to the supermarket. It was a long walk and she was getting tired. A taxi came along and she decided to take the taxi to the supermarket. Taxis also run on the barter system and by this time she felt comfortable enough to try her hand at bartering. We had discussed the pricing the night before so she had a general idea what the service was worth. She negotiated a fair price for the ride. When they arrived at the supermarket the taxi driver would not take her money – he said she could give him a ride if he ever came to Canada! Once again, she was in awe. Those incidents are a true testament to the generosity and hospitality Omanis extend to guests in their country.

One night in March, Jackey and I attended our first symphony concert in Oman. It was wonderful! I had wanted to go for a very long time, but whenever a concert was scheduled, I had company from Canada and was not able to attend. The one we finally went to was a special concert, held at the Crowne Plaza Hotel, one of the tourist hotels in Oman. My ticket cost ten rials, or about $30, the standard price of a symphony ticket in Muscat. The special concert was in honour of the maestro's son, who was visiting Muscat from London. The performance took place in one of the hotel ballrooms.

The audience consisted almost entirely of expats, with a few Omanis in attendance. Most of the attendees were Caucasian and over fifty. The first time I attended that type of function in Muscat I was overwhelmed to be in a room with that many expats. But I've become accustomed to that crowd and expect it at the dinner theatres and concerts that came through town. This was your typical symphony group, some in blue jeans and some in tuxes. Almost everyone was dressed up a bit, though not in formal attire – the men in suits and the ladies in dresses.

The dress of the orchestra members was very pleasing to the eye. The men wore tuxedos, instead of their traditional dishdashas and hats. It was so different to see the hair on Arab men's heads! The women wore traditional Oman outfits. The clothing is different from region to region, and the ladies were dressed in Muscat-region outfits: green pants, green tunics, and red sheylas (head scarves), with the traditional gold jewellery headband. What a pleasing contrast, the black, red, and green.

I was curious about the Royal Oman Symphony Orchestra for a couple of reasons: I wondered what the quality of the performance would be like, and was very curious about the program. I overheard one of the audience members say during the intermission – a man from the UK, I believe – that one of the things he loved about the ROSO was you never knew what you were going to hear. He continued, saying that, at home, the program always pretty predictable, and he really enjoyed the variety of this young orchestra. That was certainly true of the event Jackey and I attended. We were treated to a lively combination of pieces, from Tchaikovsky's ballet music to *My Fair Lady*. I was delighted. The maestro's son provided us with some impressive trumpet performances.

I looked forward to another concert in April, when the orchestra would be back in its regular venue, the Al Bustan Hotel. That hotel is owned by the Sultan and has just undergone a fourteen-million-dollar renovation. I expected it would be quite lovely. The Sultan is also building a very large opera house in Muscat. I hope I will be in Oman long enough to enjoy a concert there.

As I mentioned earlier, I belong to the American Women's Group here in Oman. A great piece of advice given to me by my British friend, Sandra, who has lived in Oman for twenty-five years: join, join, join! So I became a member not only of the American Women's Group (www.awgoman.com), which is part of a world-wide organization, but also the Women's Guild of Oman, which is mostly British. No, there is not a Canadian women's group, nor any sort of Canadian group, but the ones I've joined kindly accept Canadians and other nationalities.

There is one event every year in March that is put on mostly by Canadians, called the Canadian Stampede. I decided to serve on the organizing committee. The Stampede is an offshoot of the Petroleum Development Oman group, the largest petroleum development and production company in Oman (www.pdo.co.com). It's a very large and complex organization, and as far as I can figure out, there is a Canadian club associated with the PDO recreational facility. I'm not sure about the number of Canadians working for PDO, but I met some very nice fellow Canadians while serving on the committee.

The Canadian Stampede is a take-off on the Calgary Stampede, of course. It's a great evening out. We take over the badminton courts at the PDO recreation centre and convert it into a fabulous outdoor venue, complete with a mechanical bull ride, outdoor stage, and hay bales. A DJ is brought in from Calgary for the event, which consists of a buffet meal, dance lessons, lots of dancing, a shooter bar, and a regular bar. A draw is held, and the first prize is airfare and entry to the real Calgary Stampede. The biggest job for this event is setting up the venue. It takes about twenty people the full day to prepare the site. The advantage of serving on the committee is the availability of tickets. Tickets for this event sell like hotcakes. The first sale is for Canadian's only, and the initial 200 tickets sell in about twenty minutes. A few weeks later there is another sale for all nationalities; those tickets also sell in about twenty minutes. People start to line up early. If you're on the committee, you get two tickets for your time and the option to purchase four more without standing in line – a huge bonus!

The American Women's Group supports local charities with their fundraising events. They also do a great job of organizing trips and events to connect the expat and the Omani populations. Many expat women in Oman have no contact with the Omani people. Women who come to Oman under their husbands' sponsorships are not allowed to hold jobs, so their exposure to the local people and culture is often limited to what they experience in the grocery stores and malls. In March of 2009, the AWG staged an "Omani Night." The event was hosted at the Omani Women's Association, and they provided valuable content and contacts. I was able to attend only part of the event, as Jackey and I were off to Thailand that night and could not stay long. Traditional Omani food was served, and a traditional wedding ceremony was portrayed.

But the organizers arranged an interesting pre-event to Omani Night. An American woman, married to an Omani gentleman and a long-time resident of Oman, shared her expertise on traditional Omani costumes. First, we went to the American Club for a lecture. She took us through the different regions of Oman and the different traditional costumes associated with the regions – it was fascinating. I remembered the wedding we attended when we first arrived and how our friend Fatma identified for us where the women were from by their dress. After the lecture, we all drove down to the souq and were guided through the local shops. Our hostess took us to different shops that sold the traditional dress of different areas. I saw parts of the souq that I did not even know existed. It was an exotic adventure, winding through narrow streets and alleyways: the fragrance of *bakhoor* (incense) burning; the bright coloured silks, satins, and cottons; the Arabic language being spoken. It was so much fun! Jackey and I did not purchase an outfit that evening for the big event coming up, but later we shopped at a trade event and purchased a Balushi (tribe name) outfit; mine was bright yellow and Jackey's plum-coloured. I have since purchased another Balushi outfit, much fancier. I still need to get it sewn up to my measurements. Perhaps I will get invited to a Balushi wedding and have an opportunity to wear it.

Just to give you an idea of some other events put on by the women's groups:

AWG hosts a Halloween party and a Christmas bazaar where you can buy homemade gifts, jewellery, carpets, paper products, etc., some just like home (angels for your tree, butter tarts, and shortbread cookies) and some local. This year I ran a Story Board group for them. It was such a success, the five ladies who came want to continue to meet on a monthly basis. We will continue with personal development exercises and have some fun. There are not many events for women such as myself who have day-jobs, since most of the club events are in the daytime, so evening events are well received.

The Women's Guild (www.womensguildoman.org) puts on the Crystal Ball, a charity fundraiser, which I wrote about earlier. This is their big event of the year. In addition they put on smaller events throughout the season (October to April). The best service they provide is sending out a daily email that lists events in Muscat. It's your connection to the city. That's how I found out about the symphony and other events about town. It's very difficult to find out about such things without that service. The newspapers usually have a write-up after the event is over – very frustrating, but WG saves the day.

They also host regular coffee mornings with speakers; but again, if you work, you are out of luck, unless you have some flexibility in your schedule.

Both AWG and WG, but particularly WG, provide an extensive list of business partners that offer members discounts. I have had expat men ask how they can become members just for the discounts!

Thailand – medical student on the train.

A trip to Thailand

One of my personal goals during my time in the Middle East was to travel to destinations on that side of the world; thus, the trip to India in December, and then in March, five glorious days in Thailand. Jackey was going and she invited me to accompany her. I am glad I made the decision to go, especially as it was so nice to have a travel companion with whom to share the experience. Jackey would be leaving Oman before I did, and I realized how much I would miss her.

Thailand was a surprise. I had heard so many things about the country that I was a little leery about my trip there. As most people know, Thailand has a reputation for its sex trade, especially its very young sex workers. I now think it's unfortunate that this is the automatic association with Thailand. The land is beautiful and the people very friendly; it's called "The Land of Smiles." I am sure if you go to Thailand looking for the sex trade you will find it; in fact, I am pretty sure you will find it in any country. However, that was not the purpose of our trip, and I am happy to report that we discovered another side of Thailand.

We arrived in Bangkok early in morning after flying all night on a very crowded plane, so rest was the first thing on our schedule. We stayed at a five-star hotel and certainly enjoyed its luxuries – a hot bath with bath salts, comfortable beds, and fresh fruit in the room. That evening we had a dinner cruise booked. Bangkok at night! – very crowded and noisy; but we still enjoyed the cruise and the meal. It gave us a good overview of the city. The dock was conveniently located next to a shopping mall full of silk material and artwork. I purchased a silk blouse and had a crepe skirt made to go with it. They delivered the blouse and the skirt to my hotel the next day. What a luxury! Bangkok is a thriving, cosmopolitan city and very inexpensive to visit. We were quite surprised at the low prices

The next day we took a city tour. Oh-my-god!

(When my sister was visiting me in Oman, we overheard a group of tour guides mimicking tourists who say, "Oh-my-god." The tour guides kept repeating this in high-pitched voices and laughing. They did not know we were watching until we began to laugh very loudly also. Later, we shared the story with Jackey, and we all agreed, we *never* use that phrase. Ha-ha...)

In Bangkok, when we saw all the intricate architecture, our most common expression was, "Oh-my-god!" And then we would chuckle to ourselves and say we didn't care, because those places really were incredible. We visited the Royal Palace and Temples. Our tour guide's name was Bhat; she was a lovely Thai lady. When she took us around, Jackey and I were so awestruck with the first building, we spent about half an hour just enjoying the stunning design. Bhat kept trying to get us moving, but we were very busy enjoying that amazing building. Suddenly we looked around us and realized there were about twenty other buildings of equal opulence and beauty. We began to laugh as we realized our short-sightedness. After that, we listened more attentively to Bhat.

The first Royal Palaces were constructed in 1782 by King Rama I, with additions made by each successive King. King Rama V, between 1868 and 1910, made significant additions to the palaces. The Emerald Buddha is housed on those grounds also. The Emerald Buddha dates back to 1434 and is carved from jade. It was moved to its home on the palace grounds in 1784. The statue is sixty-six cm high and about forty-eight cm wide at the lap. There are three gold costumes for the Emerald Buddha to wear: one for summer, one for the rainy season, and one for winter. Incredible! The history and beauty of this area leave one breathless.

We had lunch at a small outdoor café, under an umbrella, as by this time the sun was very hot. We enjoyed an authentic Thai meal and purchased dessert from a street vendor beside the restaurant. Bhat explained to us what it was: sweet coconut rice wrapped in a banana leaf – delicious! We sampled the street food quite often during our time in Bangkok and the surrounding areas. It was all very good, much better than eating at a restaurant, and there was lots of variety. The streets are lined with vendors selling fresh fruits and vegetables, juices in coconut shells, and Thai delicacies. I would highly recommend the street food to anyone visiting Bangkok.

We purchased parasols to protect us from the sun for the rest of the day, and in the afternoon we explored a different part of Bangkok, the water canals. Originally there were over 300 canals throughout the city, supporting the rich agricultural community. Today there remain about a hundred of these canals. We enjoyed a calm, peaceful boat-ride ride down one of them. We stopped at a temple that's in charge of taking care of the fish in the canal.

We purchased food for the fish and then fed them off the side of the boat. Hundreds of fish came right up to us to get a tasty morsel.

The homes along the river were posh, with lots and lots of plants and trees, quite the contrast to the deserts of Oman. Overall, Bangkok is a lush and attractive city, but particularly so along the canals. One couldn't help but wonder what life would be like living beside one of those waterways, enjoying the warm days. We got lots of smiles and waves from the residents of the homes as they went about their daily chores.

Bhat instructed our driver to drop us off at the Night Market. There I experienced my first Thai massage. A one-hour massage cost $10, and what a massage! I had been having difficulty with my back, and that massage therapist fixed it completely. He twisted and turned me like a pretzel. I was very tired afterwards, but relieved to be rid of the back pain and discomfort. I got hooked on Thai massage. Jackey chose reflexology and found it quite satisfying.

Then, we explored the market. We found a great little restaurant to enjoy another fabulous Thai meal. After that we attempted to shop a bit, but discovered we were very, very tired – our shopping effort was minimal. So we took a *tuk-tuk* home to our hotel. What a great way to travel in the city! A tuk-tuk is a small, open-air, three-wheeled, motorized vehicle. The driver can scoot in and out of traffic. We hired a tuk-tuk every time we could from then on – what fun!

Day Four in Bangkok proved to be very different from the first three. Bhat and our driver picked us up for a two-hour drive. Our destination: the train station, where we would begin a trip alongside the River Kwai. At the station, there is a railway bridge spanning the river and we walked across it – a serene experience, I would say; but there is also a gentle energy about the place. The area is famous for its World War II history, but we decided to focus on that element of history on a future visit, and skipped the cemeteries and war sites this time.

I must try to paint this picture for you: Jackey and I are walking towards the bridge that crosses the historic River Kwai. The scene is quiet, serene, lush with trees and lovely flowers, and includes a small market. As we enter the market, we are greeted by one of the local vendors with his boom box blasting the song, "Play That Funky Music White Boy." Jackey and I laughed so hard – what a contrast! We continued on through the market, but "Play that Funky Music White Boy" didn't leave us; we found ourselves singing and humming snippets from it throughout the rest of our holiday.

Jackey and I purchased some cotton skirts to help alleviate the heat. What a great investment – we wore those skirts every day for the rest of the trip. I expect they will also serve as the central part of my wardrobe once the heat of summer is upon us in Oman. We also purchased fresh coconut juice, and then made our way back to the terminal. There we ran into about sixteen local students from an English-language camp. They were, I am guessing, twelve to thirteen years of age, and were out on an excursion with their two teachers. The students had workbooks with questions in English written in them. Their goal was to find English-speaking people, ask them questions, and then get the English people to sign their workbooks. They were so cute – reluctant to speak English. Boy, I could sure relate to this experience, as I am trying to learn Arabic. But they had a lot of courage, and between many giggles and shy looks, we managed to communicate fairly well. Their teachers explained the project to us, but even they had limited English and were eager to practice their conversational skills.

Another group of older students asked me to take their picture and I happily complied. They turned out to be our travelling companions on the train ride following the River Kwai. Although shy for a while, they eventually got brave and started up a conversation. I discovered they were medical students on a break after writing exams. I asked about what they would do after graduation, and they told me they would be assigned positions by the government. They each had a specialty and were in their fourth year. They were full of energy and excitement, huddling together and figuring out a question to ask me. One of them would be the spokesperson and would relay the information back to the others. Their English was limited but pretty good, and conversations were fairly easy. I really enjoyed being around them.

The train ride along the River Kwai was breathtaking. We arrived at our destination and enjoyed yet another great meal at a picturesque restaurant, surrounded by flowers, trees, and birds.

Our driver met us at the restaurant and we motored back to Bangkok. On our way we stopped at Gems Gallery. Jackey is a very good jewellery and gem shopper and has been educating me. Rubies and emeralds are the standard gems of Thailand, but every gemstone was available in that gallery. As we browsed, we were escorted by a personal shopper – a nice touch and a good sales technique. We both became paying customers. Jackey bought three rings and I bought a pearl drop pendant with matching earrings and a garnet ring. We also purchased a few silver chains. We chose a gem in a silver setting for Bhat as a gift. She was delighted.

We returned to our hotel and searched for a massage place, to no avail. We ended up taking a tuk-tuk back to the Night Market. But first we ate dinner at an outdoor restaurant. We were too tired after that for a massage, so just headed back to the hotel for a good night's sleep.

The next day we took a jaunt southwest of the city. Our first stops were a coconut farm and an orchid farm. At the coconut farm Bhat showed us how the coconut fruit is shredded and the coconut milk extracted from the fruit. We also watched a coconut sugar demonstration. The milk is drained from the coconut and then processed through three large cooking vats until it turns to sugar. The coconut sugar is then pressed into small, round patties. We taste-tested one of the samples and Jackey decided to purchase a bag of them. We proceeded to eat them like candy. When we returned to the car we offered some to Bhat and our driver. They both looked at us and exclaimed, "We use that for baking!"

Oh well, we kept eating them anyway, much to their dismay. There were small booths selling coconut shell purses and trinkets, coconut oil, which I purchased, and coconut creams and lotions scented with different flower essences – a very complete use of the coconut. I started taking the oil internally after that and found it to be a great supplement.

Next we walked over to the orchid gardens. What a variety of colours and shapes! Beautiful, beautiful, beautiful! Orchids grow everywhere in Thailand. I asked Bhat about tulips and lilies, and she said they grow up in the north of the country where it was cold. It was obvious to me that she and I had different definitions of cold.

We drove for another hour, and then took a boat ride down the country canals. They were quite different from the city canals – wider and more elaborate, with larger homes on the banks. Our captain spotted two enormous lizards basking in the sun along the shore.

Our destination was the Floating Market – an interesting place to shop, with the wares displayed in boats along the piers. The customers walk along the pier and visit the shops. Some of the boats have dry goods, some are food vendors, and some contain fresh fruit and vegetables. The colours, the sights, the sounds, and the smells are tantalizing. Jackey and I shopped a bit, but time was limited, as we still had a few more stops on this excursion, and then the long ride back to Bangkok. We browsed a bit, purchasing a few paintings and Buddha ornaments. Our next stop was the Rose Garden for lunch and a Thai cultural show. The Rose Garden includes banquet facilities, a retreat and spa centre, a cultural centre, a replica of a Thai village, and miles and miles of sculptured gardens. Incredible – orchids as far as the eye could see! Roses as far as the eye could see! The cultural show, a play depicting local culture in music and dance, was quite entertaining. It included a sword-fighting demonstration, and, of course, an elephant.

Back in Bangkok, we were dropped off at a mall where we could shop, get a massage, and have something to eat. We ended up in the food court again, but once more we had a fine meal. We chuckled at this, finding food-court food so enjoyable, but it was. We stopped to purchase some luggage at a small shop. Jackey bought two gigantic suitcases, which she needed for her trip home to Canada. For the rest of the evening we wheeled those suitcases around, in and out of the many small shops in the mall. It was quite hilarious. But they came in handy for carrying our purchases of the day. We both went for a wonderful Thai massage and thoroughly enjoyed ourselves. We did a bit more shopping, but it was late and most of the stores were closed. We found our way to the taxi location, stood in a long line-up, and finally got a tuk-tuk home. The driver strapped the big suitcases onto the back of the vehicle and we were off. What a great way to travel!

On our last day in Thailand we woke up to rain – soft, gentle rain. Oh, it was delightful! Unfortunately, our schedule for the day involved an open-air market that operated only on that particular day of the week. So instead, we explored Chinatown a bit, then returned to the big mall we'd been at the day before. All the shops were open this time, so we browsed to our heart's content.

Then it was off to the airport. I was hoping for another massage before we left, but there just wasn't enough time…

Thailand is a country that I plan to visit again. We spent all our time in Bangkok and surrounding areas. But there are two more trips now calling to me: one to explore the northern part of the country – the mountainous Chiang Mai area – and one to visit the southern part of Thailand – Phuket, with its fabulous beaches and islands. I am so glad I got to travel in that part of the world.

The goat souq in Nizwa.

Again, the goat

In the spring of 2009, I started taking Arabic language lessons. At my first class I met a lady from India whose name was also Benita. That was the first time in my life I had met another Benita. She even spelled it *Benita*, not *Bonita*. She had been living in Oman for twenty years and was applying for citizenship, which meant she needed to be able to speak Arabic. Imagine going all the way to Oman to meet someone with the same name as yours! There were ten students in the class. My friend Judith, originally from Calgary, also attended. Surprisingly, there was another lady in the class named Judith, an English teacher from Halifax. This caused quite a bit of confusion for our Sudanese instructor. Other classmates were two young Arab women from America; football players; an army officer from Wales; a young lady from America, who was also a teacher; two gentlemen from India; a young lady from Pakistan who was accompanying her husband on his posting to Oman; and an Omani woman of African descent who spoke Swahili and English, but no Arabic – an eclectic bunch!

It was June before I finally experienced significant rain in Muscat – about thirty minutes worth one evening. That was the first time in a year that I had heard rainfall outside my window. There had been a few showers here and there, but none that lasted any length of time. Listening to the rain that night was a big treat for me. It reminded me of spring mornings when the rain comes and everything starts to turn green as new life sprouts from the ground and the trees. I went outside after the rain stopped, expecting the familiar smell of fresh, clean, cool air that we have in Canada after a rainfall. But I was surprised to be met instead by a sultry, humid evening. The rain was wonderful, but sure created havoc on the roads. I needed to be somewhere that evening, and it took an extra forty-five minutes to arrive at my destination. As

101

there is no drainage system here, the water just sits on the roads in low-lying areas and creates chaos with traffic. C'ést la vie!

Canadians are such rule followers, so an incident that happened in June was a crisis for me – MY WORST NIGHTMARE! – with a happy ending.

When I first arrived in Muscat, my colleagues used to laugh at me because I was so worried about driving with my Canadian driver's license and not knowing if that was legal or not (a piece of information that I could mysteriously not find out). I arrived in April, 2008, and it took until October to get my Oman license. I needed a Canadian license that was valid for six months, but since I received my residence card only in July, and my Canadian license expired in October, I did not meet the six-month requirement. When I returned to Canada in the summer of my first year in Oman, I renewed my Canadian license. However, it was an early registration, so I had to wait until October, when my license was actually due, before it was mailed to me.

Well, I was very relieved and happy when I finally had both my Oman residence card and my Oman driver's license. As I mentioned earlier in the book, Talal had registered both my car and the insurance in the company name. Mid-May 2009, I received an urgent text from Talal saying my insurance had expired May 1 and to get down to the insurance office as soon as possible. I did so immediately. Bit of a complication as the car was still registered in the company's name. But Talal knew the insurance guy and worked it all out for me. Talal offered to do the transfer; I just needed to bring him the yellow piece of paper necessary for registration, along with the insurance papers. I turned the documents over to Talal. I told him that the date on the yellow card was August, 2008. (It was the only part written in English, the rest was in Arabic.) He assured me that he had registered the vehicle for a one-year period.

But now when Talal went to transfer the registration, it turned out that my car had not been registered since *August, 2008*!! Yikes, no insurance and no registration for almost a year! My worst nightmare…

On top of that, I was asked upon renewal whether or not I wanted coverage for the United Arab Emirates as well. I was very surprised that I did not have coverage for the UAE. I had by that time made eight trips to Dubai, all with no car insurance! Oh-my-God!

I was ecstatic when I was finally able to say that I had a vehicle that I knew was insured and registered both in Oman and the UAE. I sometimes wonder what would have happened had I been in an accident or been pulled over by the police, but I don't wonder long. Those thoughts are quickly replaced with feelings of extreme gratitude for having been safe over that period, and extreme comfort in knowing that I am covered on all bases now.

Once, I went on a business trip to Salalah, about 1,000 km south of

Muscat, but still in Oman. Salalah has about 250,000 residents. It's rainy season lasts two months. The city gets more than a million visitors during that time, mostly from the Gulf countries and Europe.

The branch manager picked me up at the airport and was my host for the two days. At the end of the second day, after I had finished my interviews, we went out for lunch before heading back to the airport.

He drove to a special place – not a restaurant – where six men were working intently over a fire pit. My host was very excited to take me there. He said it was the best meat, the babies. I asked for clarification and he told me he was talking about baby goats. Okay – I could almost deal with that, would try and be a good guest and at least sample some of the meat. Just as that thought went through my head, didn't he just have to go and point out that they were at that very moment bringing in another kid for slaughter? I looked, and there was the cutest little baby goat, wrapped up in a blanket, being carried to the slaughter room!

Inside I was screaming, but I remained outwardly calm. We waited quite a while for the meat to cook, then it was brought to us in a package of tin foil. My companion threw the package in the back seat of his SUV, and I thought I had been saved; I wasn't going to have to eat it after all.

HA!

We proceeded to a restaurant, and he brought the package of meat in with us! He asked for an extra plate and began to happily eat the meat. Several times he invited me join him. After the third or fourth time, I accepted and somehow choked it down. I said I simply could not eat anymore, and my fellow diner accepted that.

I can still see that cute little baby goat...

My friend Habib in Dubai (that's not his boat!).

Dubai, and Arabian nights

As I got to know Dubai better, I started liking it more and more. At first, it was just another large city with more than its share of tourist attractions. After about the fourth trip to Dubai with guests visiting from Canada, it even began to get boring: city tour; evening cruise on a dhow, with dinner; and of course, the obligatory desert safari.

But on my very first trip there, I met a tour guide named Habib. He was wonderful, a very gentle and kind soul, originally from Bangladesh. We became immediate friends. Every time I went to Dubai with guests, Habib was our guide. His sweet nature added a nice contrast to that very busy and congested city – a special treat for my Canadian friends. I kept in touch with him and visited him in Dubai even when I did not have company. It's interesting to experience his culture through his eyes. He spends six months in Dubai and six months back home with his family. And of course, he sends quite a bit of his money home to his parents to help with family.

As I said, I grew to like Dubai more and more as the year passed, and in spring, Jackey and I visited the city for the first time together and with no guests in tow. Habib picked us up at the airport and we enjoyed dinner with him. Then we went to a new hotel on the city outskirts, close to one of the very large malls. Yes, I said, *one* of the very large malls. A tour guide we met joked about the malls, calling Dubai, "Do Buy." This particular mall had 800 stores and was close to the latest and greatest new mall that has 1200 stores – do buy! Shopping there is equivalent to shopping in London or Paris, but Jackey and I still preferred the souqs. Dubai has an enormous Gold Souq – precious gems, gold, and some silver. With Jackey teaching me how to shop for precious stones and gold, I came to own a few key pieces.

The next day was a leisurely day of shopping at the souqs – Gold Souq, Traditional Souq, and Spice Souq. The smells in a souq are tantalizing. Many of the shops burn Arabian *oud,* a distinct and provocative smell. I burn oud on a regular basis at my Muscat home. It is heavenly.

The trip to Dubai was a going-away gift for Jackey. She does a lot of shopping, so I wanted to give her an experience gift rather than a material one. With that in mind, I chose for her a performance of Cirque du Soleil. I had always wanted to attend one of the shows in Las Vegas, but could never get tickets. This was a wonderful opportunity and we were not disappointed. The performance was memorable.

The next day we enjoyed a leisurely breakfast and went to the mall. Lunch was *dim sum,* which we hadn't had since being in Oman. There are many benefits to a larger city, along with the drawbacks of traffic and congestion. Dubai is quite different from Oman. Oman is still Omani – eighty percent of the people dress in traditional Omani dress, dishdashas for the men and abayas for the ladies. The Omani people live and work in their country; they are the majority of the population. Dubai is only approximately eighteen percent UAE Nationals. Rarely do you see a dishdasha or an abaya. Strange how westernized it is. One of my Omani clients was most offended one day when he saw a picture of the current ruler of Dubai wearing a gold necklace. This is strictly forbidden in the Muslim tradition.

We were scheduled to return home the day after the show. Habib had to work during the day, but picked us up later in the afternoon to take us to the airport.

I once spent a weekend in Dubai strictly to hang out with Habib. We went for dinner and a movie. There are movie theatres in Oman, too – three, to be exact. In Dubai, however, the theatres are modern, with big screens and Surround-Sound. Not sure those things make for a better movie, but the selection of films is certainly broader. We enjoyed tea at an outdoor café along the famous Dubai Creek.

Both of those experiences showed me a different Dubai, a diverse and quieter city, away from the tourist noise. It was nice to enjoy a leisurely time in a city famous for its tourist attractions. The tourist attractions are amazing, but I want you to know there is more to the city than the tallest- and largest-everything in the world!

My son and I one time took a trip to Dubai to take in an international football match. Habib was at home in Bangladesh with his family at the time, and it did seem strange to be there without seeing him. Nevertheless, Joey was thrilled to be watching some of the best soccer players in the world: Germany vs. UAE. Germany won, but it was not a hands-down loss for the UAE, as was expected, and we both enjoyed the game. The experience was interestingly different from attending football in Oman.

One time when Joey and I decided to go to a friendly game in Oman, I had to go to my Arabic class first and planned to join Joey later. In Oman the men and women are separated at the game, but Joey didn't realize that until later. He enjoyed himself before I arrived, sitting with the men. One of the Omanis befriended him and helped him out whenever required. Joey sent me a text-message saying, "Mom, there are no women here, so if you don't want to come, you don't need to. I am okay." By the time I got the text I was already at the stadium. I sent him a text and he met me outside. When we tried to access the seat he'd been using previously, the guards wouldn't let us in. We couldn't figure out at first what the heck was going on. Finally, one of the guards who spoke some English said, "Family section, family section." A light bulb went on – of course, the women cannot sit with the men! We finally found the family section and took our seats with the families. There were still about fifteen minutes left in the game. There is no such segregation in Dubai.

One of the things I really liked about attending sporting events in both Oman and Dubai, is that no alcohol is allowed, making the crowd much more civilized; no constant stream of foul language and calls for blood from the fans, which is much more to my liking. Same uncomfortable bleachers to sit on, though...

All in all, it is nice to be close enough to a major city like Dubai to take advantage of the wider range of offerings, and still be able to come back to quiet little Muscat to live. The best of both worlds!

About the Dubai desert safari I mentioned earlier: it consists of dune-bashing in a 4x4, followed by an Arabian dinner in a Bedouin tent, complete with belly dancer, henna tattoos, camel ride, and having your picture taken with a falcon on your arm, all under the exquisite Arabian night sky. I took visitors from home on this touristy little adventure several times.

One of the highlights of the desert safari was our driver. He dressed and looked like an Arab, but I found out that he was actually from Bangladesh. He kept us entertained with stories about his life, his parents, his brothers and sisters. He had graduated as a chemical engineer because that is what his father had expected, but he found the work really boring. So he bought a 4x4 and starting conducting desert safaris. He was a rebel driver, bringing up the rear in the cavalcade of 4x4s out in the desert, always taking the dune not attempted by others. He was an expert driver and he thrilled us many times over. "Oh my God!" was commonly heard from us tourists as we swept over the dunes, often on two wheels with sand spraying out in a graceful arc beside us. In his opinion, this driving was easy; the real challenge came when driving in the desert at night. We were lucky enough to experience that returning from the Bedouin tent in the late evening. He gave us a good sample of his night driving abilities, equally breathtaking. One time, my friend Linda from

Saskatchewan asked him if the police ever came out into the desert to stop him. He laughed uproariously. He looked at her with a twinkle in his eye and said, "They could never catch me. I know this desert like the back of my hand." Oh, he was a feisty young man!

I recently joined a group of expats going out to do a beach clean up, a save-the-environment kind of activity, consisting of fourteen Frenchmen, two Omanis, one Brit, and myself. We drove to Ras Al Haad, about three hours southwest of Muscat, though still in Oman. The drive along miles and miles of unspoilt beach and coastline was lovely. I have been told that there is a plan to put thirty-seven hotels along that stretch of coast in the near future, which made me feel quite sad, actually. Progress? But I did appreciate the new four-lane divided superhighway along the coastline. Prior to the highway being built, you needed a 4x4 vehicle to access these roads less travelled, or you would have had to cross the desert, which at least had a paved road; but the journey would have taken an hour longer.

We spent the first day cleaning up the beach – a couple of hours' work and it was spotless. The beach was located in a tiny cove of pristine waters where the Indian Ocean and the Gulf of Arabia meet. We went for a swim after the clean-up, while our hosts prepared a barbecue for us. The meal was potluck, so we had quite a variety: fruits and salads, and lamb, beef, and chicken cooked on the open fire. And, of course, some very thoughtful soul brought chocolate cake. Ah, the pure luxury of it all!

Three of us ladies decided to sleep on the beach overnight. Jane was a nurse instructor from Sohar, two hours north of Muscat. She was from the UK originally. She had come to Muscat with her husband and daughter. The daughter was attending university in the UK. The husband had started sleeping with the housemaid, and Jane was now on her own and not too happy about it. She was, however, determined to make the best of her new life and we enjoyed her down-to-earth manner and gentle humour. Donna was also from the UK. She'd worked for the UN for a good part of her career and had fascinating stories to share. Like myself, she was thinking of writing a book about her experiences. Every time I see her, I am reminded of our conversations about book-writing. She is presently working for a British general in Oman.

I had brought a sleeping bag, but did not need it initially. Temperatures were around 38–39oC. When the wee hours of the morning came with the breeze off the water, I was extremely glad to have some cover. Funny how quickly you become adjusted to the temperatures. But I now understand why, when people talk about the Arabian nights, their eyes glaze over: the stillness, the apparent emptiness, the star-filled night sky, the warm breezes coming off the clear temperate waters… Sleeping on a beach overnight on the edge of the desert is a spiritual experience.

The next day was spent in leisurely enjoyment of the beach. One of our hosts, a Frenchman originally from South America, climbed out onto the rocks and harvested the oysters clinging to the cliffs. He knew exactly how to harvest them, watching for the very tiny opening in the shell which was his chance to enjoy the fresh oyster inside. There is a species of bird here that has a bill shaped just right to get into the shells of the oysters. It was quite a learning experience for me. About every hour or so, a fishing boat would come by to scoop up the schools of sardines swimming about. The sardines were fun to watch. We would wade out into the water about waist deep and get in the middle of the school, the little fish swimming around us. At first, they appeared to be a large dark mass, but when you got closer you could see the sun shining off silver bodies. The fishes were all sizes and colours – yellow, black, blue, and white – and all were visible to the naked eye. We caught a glimpse of an occasional eel, though they were very shy and swam away quickly. We spent the better part of the day discovering the riches in these waters.

Back on shore later in the day, I was witness to the "crab dance." I didn't notice the crabs until Donna pointed them out. As we sat very, very still on the beach, they began to emerge from their homes in the sand. The battle for territory began, each one scooping up piles of sand with its pincers to create mounds around its home, and every now and again advancing on another crab to let him know where the boundaries lay. I was in awe, watching this performance. But you had to be very still and quiet, for as soon as there was any motion or noise, they would retreat, and the beach would become a quiet, uninhabited stretch of sand. Donna was a wealth of information about the life around us, the birds, fish, and insects. At one point during the clean-up one of the Omani men discovered a scorpion. He was going to kill it, but our French hosts stopped him. We never saw the scorpion again, but it did make me wonder about sleeping out in the open on the beach!

The smell wafting in from a salt-water sea is unique, too. It's hard to describe – not the fresh, clean smell of fresh-water bodies, but almost a sultry, intoxicating aroma. It invites you to just set yourself down, enjoy the warm breeze blowing over your skin, and to come in for a light, buoyant dip whenever you are ready. Lying on the beach that day, I was reminded of the endless days of sunshine and warm temperatures this climate afforded. As I looked out over the water, I was tantalized by the bounty of colours: the turquoise waters, the deep blue sky, the craggy rocks and their shades of blacks, browns, beiges, and whites, and, of course the pristine sand. Life in Oman is so easy, easy on the eyes, easy on the body, and easy on the soul.

Gazing at the sparkling seawaters I found it hard to imagine there could ever be stress. I felt once more that overwhelming peace and gratitude so familiar to me now, and I lay back to simply enjoy all of it...

Jackey and me.

Epilogue

As I relax in one of the sitting rooms in my villa now, and look around at my home, I realize how comfortable I am. Yes, comfortable, a new word for me to apply to my life in Muscat. It has been over a year since I arrived in this once strange land. I have had many wonderful experiences and adventures here. I hope to have many more.

Things have certainly changed. My co-worker Jackey has left for Canada. She did not renew her contract, as her children and husband returned to Canada in November, 2008. She completed her work and has now returned to be with her family. Although I dearly miss her, I also accept that things will not remain the same. It was difficult at first to imagine being in Muscat by myself. Jackey and I came to this city together, delivered the first three contracts for the Achievement Centre, explored, discovered, laughed, and cried together. We found homes, furniture, cars, and friends. The most important gift I received from Jackey was the gift of laughter. Many times in the past year I have been so grateful to be here with someone who has such a great sense of humour. We were able to see the humour in many of the absurd situations we found ourselves in. Many of these situations I have shared with you in this book. Remember the three-hour drive back and forth between the UAE and Oman border to renew our visas?

As Jackey and I completed the first contracts for the Achievement Centre Middle East, we learned a lot in the process, established a very good reputation for the company, and formed many wonderful business relationships. The people of Oman are a gentle and respectful people, a pure joy to work with. Their level of integrity is truly inspiring in the sometimes not so integral global business world. I am forever grateful to Dr. Mohammed Benayoune for giving me the opportunity to come to Oman and help start his business here. Mohammed is a great visionary and leader. He said the first few times we met that he was looking for a certain kind of person to bring to Oman, a mature person. (Notice he was sensitive enough not to say, "an older person!") I admire his courage in leaving Jackey and me alone in Oman to deliver the contracts he'd set up. He always stayed in touch and we regularly shared emails discussing progress, obstacles, and successes.

I did renew my contract, and will now forge a relationship with a new co-worker here, a coach from Austria, originally from Boston. She has lived in many places in the world because her husband works for the Austrian embassy. I am truly looking forward to working with her over the next year.

I have passed my first level of Arabic and am very excited about continuing my education in the Arabic language, reading, writing and speaking. What an opportunity to learn another language! I am so excited that I can now recognize some of the spoken words and a little of the written words.

My son has joined me and is currently looking for work. It's a blessing for me to have him here, for which I am very grateful. He has joined a rugby team and is practising in the evenings when the summer temperatures dip all the way down to 39oC. Yikes! He does have a lot of fortitude and perseverance, or, as one of my Omani clients so aptly stated, "He is a strong lad!"

I have moved to a larger space: three bedrooms, three bathrooms, two sitting rooms, kitchen, and dining room – much better. I came to Oman with two suitcases and now I have a fully furnished, three-bedroom flat, the top floor of a villa. It doesn't take long. I bought a lot of Jackey's furniture when she left, another blessing for me. I even have extra furniture and accessories now and am hoping when we bring more staff from Canada they will willingly take it. If not, I'll donate it to charity.

I still have the travel bug. I am off to Tuscany for a ten-day conference soon and will take some time to explore Italy while I'm there.

I get many questions from my friends and family back in Canada about the political situation in Oman. Although I don't know the sultan personally, I admire the foresight and vision he has maintained throughout his reign over the country.

As I look around at the modern, peaceful country I am reminded that forty years ago there were only two km of paved roads in Oman, no schools, no hospitals, no cars, no cities. Forty years ago there were Jebeli people living in the mountains supporting themselves by raising goats, donkeys, and camels, in addition to growing fruits and vegetables; the coastal peoples of Oman sustained themselves through fishing; the Bedouin, or desert people, lived in tents and traded throughout the region. Sultan Qaboos Bin Ali settled the civil wars and the threats of war from Oman's neighbor, Yemen. There has been peace in this country for the past forty years, no easy task to accomplish, as Oman has a rich history of civil wars. (If readers are interested in understanding more about Oman from an historical perspective, I recommend a fine book titled, *In the Service of the Sultan,* by Ian Gardiner.)

This astounding growth and development has been complemented with an equal growth and development of the Omani people. Oman citizens were given the opportunity to study abroad and come back to Oman to contribute to the country. In my work I hear this repeatedly from young Omanis, and I detect a passion to repay their country for the opportunities they have been given. Credit goes to the current sultan. I was raised in a democratic political country, and I was very curious about the effects of a dictatorship. I can certainly understand how a bad sultan could ruin the country and the people, draining its resources and wealth. Fortunately, the current sultan seems to be using the resources of the country not to build his personal wealth, but to build a country safe and prosperous for its people.

I have spoken to many expats and Arabs in the past year, and the overwhelming opinion is that Oman is one of the nicest countries in the Gulf. I affirm this statement loudly – Oman is a country of peace, tranquillity, and beauty. With 1200 km of unspoiled sandy beaches, warm waters, and a continuous supply of sunny days, it is pretty hard to beat. Add to this astounding natural beauty, the gentle and respectful nature of the Omani people and you have a winning combination. Sometimes I wonder if I should pinch myself just be make sure I am not dreaming. I wonder how long it will last? Will Western ways destroy this jewel in the rough? Will tourism encroach upon the natural splendour of Oman's unspoiled coastline with monstrous hotels? I secretly pray not!

Each evening I go up to my terrace and watch the sun set over the mountains. The mountains cloaked in darkness are alluring in their mystery. Just in front of the mountains are three spires from the Grand Mosque, light glowing from the inside, in contrast to the dark, looming giants behind them. The fall of night does not obscure the beauty of the whitewashed villas, which gleam even in the dim light at the end of the day. I am filled with gratitude once again for this land of peace, tranquillity, and beauty.

There are two Arabic expressions used widely throughout the Gulf and they both apply very nicely to my life in Oman:

Alhamdulillah, which means, thank God

Inshallah, which means, God willing

Alhamdulillah for this wonderful adventure, and many more to come, inshallah.

About the Author

Born and raised in Canada, Benita Stafford-Smith established a private business-coaching practice there called CoachBenita. Over a period of ten years, she established and worked with a client base she enthusiastically describes as "amazing." Benita is currently living in the Middle East and working there as an Executive Coach, continuing her lifelong passions for professional speaking, leadership training and coaching, world travel, connecting with people, and making new friends wherever she goes.

Website: www.coachbenita.com

Benita's blog: http://10timesbolder.blogspot.com

Also find Benita on Twitter, LinkedIn and Facebook